HANDBOOK FOR SOCIAL WORK WRITING

T0386493

This concise, accessible, and engaging h̲ for social work students to acquire professional and competency-based writing skills. Written by experienced educators, the book builds writing proficiency by introducing a social work-based guide to academic writing and professional communication. Each chapter addresses a specific area of social work writing and development, progressing from coursework and beginning fieldwork to practice-based assessments and reports. The authors integrate a series of scaffolded activities throughout for readers to cultivate awareness and further technique; and with sections explaining contemporary communication methods and common writing challenges, readers will be prepared to use technology both to strengthen their writing and to ease the overall process.

Excellent for use in courses across the social work curriculum and as a personal guide, the *Handbook for Social Work Writing* provides students with on-the-spot guidance for any type of academic or professional writing assignment.

Susan E. Mason, PhD, MSSW, is Professor of Social Work at the Wurzweiler School of Social Work at Yeshiva University in New York City. The author of over 40 peer-reviewed articles and multiple books, Dr. Mason has published extensively in the fields of schizophrenia, cultural diversity, health and hospital practice, and social work education. She has been editor-in-chief of *Families in Society: The Journal of Contemporary Social Services*, and has also served on other editorial boards throughout her career. On the faculty at Yeshiva University for over 20 years, Dr. Mason teaches courses in social work research, evidence-based practice, and mental health. Prior to her appointment at Yeshiva, she was a clinical social worker and researcher at Long Island Jewish Medical Center for eight years.

Wendy Zeitlin, PhD, MSW, is an Associate Professor in the Department of Social Work and Child Advocacy at Montclair State University, where she teaches writing-intensive courses in diversity, research methods, and practice-based research. Dr. Zeitlin has held academic appointments at Yeshiva University and Montclair State University. Her scholarly interests focus on public health social work with an emphasis on disabilities and access to services for historically marginalized populations. She has authored over 30 articles in peer-reviewed journals. Dr. Zeitlin is the author of *Basic Statistics for the Behavioral and Social Sciences Using R* (Oxford, 2019), and the co-author of two other titles on research methods.

HANDBOOK FOR SOCIAL WORK WRITING

Susan E. Mason and Wendy Zeitlin

Routledge
Taylor & Francis Group

NEW YORK AND LONDON

Designed cover image: Shutterstock

First published 2024
by Routledge
605 Third Avenue, New York, NY 10158

and by Routledge
4 Park Square, Milton Park, Abingdon, Oxon, OX14 4RN

Routledge is an imprint of the Taylor & Francis Group, an informa business

Library of Congress Cataloging-in-Publication Data
Names: Mason, Susan Elizabeth, author. | Zeitlin, Wendy, author.
Title: Handbook for social work writing / Susan E. Mason and Wendy Zeitlin.
Description: New York, NY : Routledge, 2024. | Includes bibliographical references and index. |
Identifiers: LCCN 2023044822 (print) | LCCN 2023044823 (ebook) |
ISBN 9780367768287 (hardback) | ISBN 9780367768270 (paperback) |
ISBN 9781003168713 (ebook)
Subjects: LCSH: Communication in social work. | Social case work reporting.
Classification: LCC HV29.7 .M376 2024 (print) | LCC HV29.7 (ebook) |
DDC 808.06/6361—dc23/eng/20231222
LC record available at https://lccn.loc.gov/2023044822
LC ebook record available at https://lccn.loc.gov/2023044823

ISBN: 978-0-367-76828-7 (hbk)
ISBN: 978-0-367-76827-0 (pbk)
ISBN: 978-1-003-16871-3 (ebk)

DOI: 10.4324/9781003168713

Typeset in Bembo
by codeMantra

CONTENTS

Introduction: Getting the Most Out of
This Handbook   1

1   Writing for Social Work Courses   4

2   Writing for the Field: Write Like a Professional
   Social Worker   25

3   Other Forms of Communication   46

4   Using Technology to Make Writing Easier   65

5   The Basics of APA Writing Style   75

6   Common Writing Challenges   94

7   Skills in Support of Critical Writing   108

Appendix A: Example of a Well-Written Paper   123
Appendix B: Commonly Used Acronyms   132
Appendix C: Sample Resume   143
References   146
Index   147

INTRODUCTION

GETTING THE MOST OUT OF THIS HANDBOOK

It is important for social workers to have good written and oral communication skills. Written communication in the form of emails or reports is often the first introduction you may have to people you will be working with—clients, agency staff, other professionals, and, as a student, professors. Strong professional writing skills help pave the way to success with your clients and your career, and make a good first impression. Alternatively, poor or ineffective writing can limit professional opportunities and could be detrimental to your clients.

This handbook is designed to provide you with the basics of effective writing as a student and, in the future, as a professional. This is not a textbook; however, it can be used to supplement your coursework. You can read through the book sequentially or refer to chapters or sections as you need them.

We deliberately set out to make the handbook flexible to use. Each chapter contains what we consider to be the most important information and skills you need to write clearly and effectively; however, we provide other resources within the handbook to help you, too. First, we provide exercises that you can complete on your own or, preferably, with a writing partner to practice skills taught in each chapter. The exercises relate to papers that you have been assigned in your own coursework and do not require the completion of worksheets or rote practice. A writing partner such as a classmate or friend who also wants to work on their writing skills is invaluable, as they can give you feedback on each of the exercises.

As we have made this handbook concise, we also provide links and/or references to other resources for each chapter that we think

DOI: 10.4324/9781003168713-1

you might find helpful. We recommend using Google or another search engine to locate each resource, as actual links may change over time.

WHAT'S IN THE HANDBOOK

We start off by addressing what is likely your most pressing need: writing for social work courses. In **Chapter 1**, we discuss why it is important to communicate effectively in writing. That is, why should you spend your time learning to be a better writer when you already have so much to do? We then move on to cultural competence in writing and additional meanings to consider in both written assignments and other types of communication. We include important points for you to consider when writing papers for your classes, including understanding what the assignment is asking you to do; identifying strategies for a well-written paper; addressing the drafting and editing of your paper; and citing published books and articles in APA 7th Edition format. **Chapter 2** expands on what we covered in Chapter 1 to consider writing as a social work professional. It contains sections on technical aspects of areas of practice, writing in charts, and creating effective process recordings and field notes, which are often required in your internships or fieldwork practice placements as a student. Sections in this chapter include writing client assessments, reports for macro-assignments, and writing clinical notes that may be used for all levels of social work education, including second-year master of social work or doctoral students. **Chapter 3** provides guidance on how to communicate effectively and professionally, including in emails, texts or direct messages, electronic meeting platforms, and letters. The chapter begins by covering helpful hints for all types of communications. Sections of this chapter then discuss effective strategies for each specific type of written and oral interaction. **Chapter 4** moves on to discuss tools and resources that are commonly used for communication. The most underutilized resource, in our experience, is your school's library; we show you how to use invaluable time-saving tools that most libraries provide to their students for free! You may already be familiar with some of the writing tools discussed in this chapter; we strive to show you features of each of these that you may not be aware of. We also provide helpful hints for improving their use in collaborations and professional writing. **Chapter 5** covers APA 7th Edition writing style, which is the expected style for use in social work published material and most student papers. The American Psychological Association's *Manual* is the source of APA 7th Edition rules for formatting manuscripts and citing the works of others. In addition to providing you with guidance on what social work students need to know, we present information and hyperlinks to selected writing tools to help you with grammar, spelling, and the structuring of ideas to enhance the professional quality of your work. Additionally, we show you how to manage and store your own papers, making them easy to retrieve for future use. In **Chapter 6**, we cover common writing challenges that even the most successful and effective communicators face from time to time. This chapter includes hints for dealing with writer's anxiety, meeting deadlines, organizing your time, and dealing with writing errors such as grammatical or punctuation mistakes. In **Chapter 7**, we discuss important concepts that are important for writing well, including critical thinking and reading. We provide suggestions on how to read commonly assigned materials—including textbooks, policy papers and research articles—for in-depth understanding. We connect these skills to the careful and effective writing that you will do throughout your career. Finally, the handbook contains three **appendices**: an example of a well-written paper which serves as a model and highlights things to consider when you are writing; a list of common abbreviations social workers use; and a model resume for an entry-level job.

In short, we hope this handbook enhances your ability to write clearly and effectively, giving you tools that are easily accessible and useful.

WRITING FOR SOCIAL WORK COURSES

WRITTEN COMMUNICATION IS IMPORTANT

Today, most students use smartphones or other electronic devices to communicate with friends, family, and other students. Text messages and emails are convenient and fast, and social media platforms enable us to communicate with those inside and outside various networks.

These platforms allow us to have virtual conversations with people using standard language, invented language, and even emojis. Over time, most users develop informal ways to convey ideas—for example, instead of, "Let me know," they write "LMK." Emojis represent a feeling or emphasize an idea. Generally, these shorthand phrases or images get ideas across quickly and with few keystrokes; friends understand the meanings.

However, when writing papers for school or process recordings for supervisors, or when contacting instructors, it is best to communicate more formally. In these situations, the informality used daily may be inappropriate because it seems unprofessional. Good written work, then, is more conventionally accepted and has well-organized ideas, good sentence structure, and correct grammar and spelling. Writing that is less formal leaves a bad impression; it may lead to poor grades and missed opportunities for employment and promotion. It can create situations where it is easy to be misunderstood. Refer to the meme on the next page. A misplaced comma can completely change the meaning of your message, leaving the reader wondering what is going on!

The reason we have written this book is to help students write well and with confidence.

DOI: 10.4324/9781003168713-2

LET'S EAT, GRANDMA.
PUNCTUATION SAVES LIVES!
Source: Adapted from Shutterstock/Hanna Schvets)

CULTURALLY RESPONSIVE COMMUNICATION

What does it mean to communicate in a culturally responsive way? Culturally responsive communication includes considering the backgrounds of the message recipients, with the intention of being sensitive to their values and preferences. It also means using words that are generally considered socially acceptable by society. This is especially important for social work students, as cultural responsiveness in written and oral communication is a central focus of social work values.

When thinking about culturally responsive writing, consider terminology, grammar, and formality. Here are helpful hints for culturally responsive writing:

- Generally speaking, when referring to race, capitalize the first letter. For example, black is a color, but Black is a race that describes a group of people.
- "People first" language is usually—although not always— preferable and refers to using adjectives to describe people, not define them. For example, a client who comes to your office in a wheelchair should not be referred to as "the wheelchair-bound man," but rather "the man who uses a wheelchair." Similarly, it is better to refer to a "child with autism" than to an "autistic child."

Sensitivity to culture and people's identities should be used in deciding the mode of communication and how to write informally or formally. Consider the following tips when planning to write:

- Avoid using idioms or slang that might not be easily understood. For example, when describing mood, "She was sad" is preferable to "She felt blue."
- When referring to people, use their preferred title pronouns (e.g., "Mr.," "Mrs.," "Ms.," "Dr.," or "Professor"), unless told otherwise.
- Be aware of how people prefer to be referred to. It is common today for people to include their preferred pronouns in their email signatures. If this is not the case, and you are unsure, you can ask by stating, "My pronouns are *she* and *her*; how would you like to be referred to?"

If you are unsure about this, ask another student or a colleague who comes from a different cultural background than your own to help you. Another set of eyes on your papers or other written communications can be useful.

Information about bias-free language is discussed in detail in Chapter 5.

WRITING FOR CLASS ASSIGNMENTS

Writing for class assignments differs from the style used for creating internship notes and reports. It also differs from the way course assignments are written in other disciplines.

Social work writing is straightforward, using active descriptors that fully illustrate situations, concepts, and theories. In addition, social work programs require students to learn and demonstrate the values of the profession—such as respecting individuals, embracing diversity, and promoting social and economic justice—in written assignments.

Writing well can lead to better grades; weak writing may send a message that class material has not been truly mastered or professional social work competency is not being met.

Planning is key in writing an assigned paper. Here are tips to conquer the writing process—the Seven Steps of Assignment Writing:

1   Carefully read the assignment to understand what the instructor is asking.
2   Manage your time and organizational skills.
3   Use scholarship such as journal articles and books or credible websites for discovery and to support your ideas.
4   Create a rough draft using your own words and use citations to acknowledge the works of others.
5   Use style guides, such as APA 7th Edition, to format papers. Additional information about APA 7th Edition can be found in Chapter 5.
6   Proofread at least once (twice or even three times is better).
7   Submit your work on the due date or before.

In this section, we will walk you through each of the above steps.

Step 1: Reading the Assignment

Although this may seem obvious, the first step when approaching a writing assignment is to understand what the instructor is asking for. Sometimes, instructors will ask questions for you to answer. Other times, they will propose a topic for an essay. In social work courses, instructors may ask for a case study or a psychosocial report. However, almost all assignments ask you to both *inform* the reader and *react* to one or more aspects of the information you provide. More information on this dual requirement is found in Chapter 7.

The type of assignment will dictate how to respond, so it is essential to read and understand the assignment thoroughly before beginning. If it is not completely clear, ask for clarification. It is better to ask a question than proceed with the wrong idea. An excellent paper that does not address what the instructor asked for will not complete the assignment correctly and may lead to a poor grade or a request to redo the paper.

It may help to read the assignment in sections. Sometimes when you understand the first part, the rest will fall into place.

Consider the following assignment examples—one for a Generalist Social Work Practice class and one for a Social Policy class:

Assignment for a Generalist Practice Course (Assignment 1)

Think of a time you asked for help to solve a personal problem. Write how you felt about the experience. What did you learn about yourself during this experience? Think about one of your clients who asked you for help with a personal problem. Describe this. Now, write how your own experience asking for help influenced how you plan to work with this client.

Discuss how both experiences relate to what you have learned in class and in your readings about social work practice.

This paper should not exceed five double-spaced pages and is due on October 1.

Assignment taken from Generalist Practice Course:
Wurzweiler School of Social Work, Yeshiva University.

Assignment for a Social Policy Course (Assignment 2)

Identify a social policy you care deeply about, but that may be controversial in some way. Examples might include immigration or drug policy. Describe the existing policy and why the issue is controversial. Use required readings from this class and other peer-reviewed sources to make the argument both for and against the existing policy. When presenting these arguments, be sure to equally represent both points of view.

Now consider your client population and discuss whether the existing policy serves your clients well or is detrimental to them.

The paper should be six to eight double-spaced pages in length. Use APA 7th Edition for your citations and provide a list of references. This should include a minimum of six references not listed in the course outline supporting your argument. The paper is due on November 8. All assignments must be uploaded to the Learning Management System.

Assignment taken from Social Policy Course:
Wurzweiler School of Social Work, Yeshiva University

Notice that in Assignment 1, the overall aim is to relate a personal experience to a professional one. Assignment 2 is quite different: it requires research into a social policy and will need more in-depth content that is best outlined in detail before beginning to write. For Assignment 2, you will need details on the selected policy for each aspect of the assignment. While you may know something about your favored position, you will need to back this up with research. The counterargument to your favored position will also need to be researched, along with evidence of how the current policy affects your client population.

The first rule in responding to assignments is to know what is being asked. If anything is unclear, be sure to seek clarification! For example, Assignment 1 reads, "Discuss how both experiences relate to what you have learned in class and in your readings about social work practice." Does this mean that class notes and required readings from the syllabus are the only expected references for this paper? Are additional outside readings required? For Assignment 2, is it clear which social policies are acceptable to consider? Can you only use national policies? What if you are personally concerned about state or local policies—would they be acceptable topics for this assignment? There is only one way to find out the answers, and that is to ask the instructor.

Writing Exercise 1.1

Working with a partner or on your own, use the following steps to review your next written assignment:

- Go over each element of the assignment and identify how you plan to respond to the assignment.
- Identify where you might look for information to meet the requirements for the assignment.
- Is there anything that you may be unsure of for this assignment? If so, do you know who to ask?
- Do one of the following:
  1 If you are working with a partner, ask for feedback. Does your partner think you can complete all aspects of this assignment given what you have told them?
  2 Brainstorm solutions if you are unsure where to look for additional information.
  3 If you are working on your own, write out the answers to the sections above, including anything you are unsure of.

Submit any additional questions about this assignment to your instructor or to your writing coach.

Step 2: Manage Your Time and Organizational Skills

In order to meet all the requirements of assignments, there are two important aspects to address: *organization* and *time*.

Starting with organization, we recommend writing an outline, even for short or seemingly easy assignments. There are several benefits of writing an outline:

- A good outline ensures that all requirements of the assignment are addressed. It can be used as a checklist of the sections that need to be covered in the response.
- Outlines help ensure that you are responding to the assignment itself and nothing else. Try not to go off on tangents. Focus on what is required.
- Outlines create headings that can be used to organize your paper. They guide the reader to the most important points you are making so that your ideas are communicated more clearly. For additional information about headings, see Chapter 5.

For example, in Assignment 1, your outline might look like this:

```
 I.   Introduction
 II.  Personal problem
      (a)  Describe the problem
      (b)  Describe asking for help
      (c)  What did you learn about yourself?
 III. Client problem
      (a)  What was the problem?
      (b)  How did they ask for help?
 IV.  Relate personal experience to client experience
 V.   How does all this pertain to class and readings?
 VI.  Conclusion
```

Notice that everything that the instructor asked for is in the outline, and all of this is presented in a logical order. In this example, we grouped all elements of the personal problem described in the assignment together, followed by all elements of the client's problem. Only after you discuss these sections separately does it make sense to analyze how the two relate each other. The end of this analysis is a good place to segue into what you have learned in class.

Also notice that we have added an introduction and conclusion to this outline. While not explicitly stated in most assignments, it is often appropriate to include a few words at the beginning to provide some context to the paper. For example, in Assignment 1, an introductory paragraph might read:

> Social workers are often asked to help clients resolve personal problems that are affecting their wellbeing and that of their families. The process of asking for help is often difficult and social workers can understand this better by looking at their own experiences of help-seeking. This paper focuses on two examples of asking for help: the first is the student's example and the second is from a client. The two are related later in the paper along with lessons learned from class presentations and readings.

This introduction explains to the reader why you are writing the paper and what to expect when reading it.

Similarly, it is also often appropriate to add a sentence or two at the end of the assignment to summarize what you have written. For example, one way to end this assignment could be as follows:

> In conclusion, the process of asking for help for personal problems may be difficult, but it can result in a positive resolution. Through course readings, this student better understands that her experience asking for help was not unusual. Additionally, she has a better understanding of the challenges that her client faced in describing her personal difficulties.

Notice that in the paragraph above, the student is referring to herself using the pronoun "her." While this may feel awkward, it is commonplace and accepted practice not to refer to yourself in the first person ("I," "my," "mine") unless your instructor permits a less formal style of writing. If in doubt, ask.

While the above are good examples of how to begin and end a paper, using your own words works best. Since you are writing the paper about yourself and your client, you are the expert on what is to be addressed in these sections. If you are unsure about what to write, you might want to save these sections for the end, after you have drafted the main sections of your assignment.

Also, notice how the outline utilizes headings, giving your work an organized appearance from beginning to end. For example, Section II concerns a *personal problem*, while Section III concerns a *client problem*. Continue to use these as section headings as you organize your paper. This will help you stay on-topic and will let your reader know what to expect next.

Now let's consider Assignment 2 further. Upon reading this assignment, it should be clear that a lot more information will need to be obtained from outside sources compared to Assignment 1. With this in mind, you might want to create an initial outline that you refine as you conduct your research for this paper. Creating a first draft of your outline will ensure that you meet all the assignment requirements even if the outline needs further revision later. Try creating an outline for this assignment on your own and then compare it to the one we prepared below:

   I. Introduction: Access to healthcare
  II. Description of the social problem: Access to healthcare
      (a) Describe the problem
      (b) Describe current policy
 III. Pros and cons
      (a) Argument for current policy
      (b) Argument against current policy
 IV. Application of current policy to client population
  V. Conclusion

Notice that we identified the social problem we intend to address in the assignment in the introduction, while the rest of the outline identifies all the elements of the assignment. Also notice that Sections II and III will likely require a great deal of outside research—much more than was required in Assignment 1.

Writing Exercise 1.2

Return to Writing Exercise 1.1.

Create an outline for completing your assignment. Ensure that your outline is comprehensive and covers all aspects of the assignment. Do one of the following:

- If you have a writing partner, provide them with a copy of your outline, and discuss where your outlines are different and where they are similar. Since you are both working on the same assignment, your outlines should be similar. Discuss what you can do to improve your outlines. Save these, as you will use them as a framework for writing your initial draft of your paper.
- If you are working on your own, make a copy of the assignment. Now, cross off each element in the assignment that you have included in your outline. When you are finished, if there is an aspect of the assignment not included in your outline, you might need to revise your outline.
- Keep in mind that the essential aspects of the outline can be easily adapted to your paper.

Managing Your Time

Students who leave written assignments until the last minute are at a distinct disadvantage. There is no way to complete an assignment well without going through the Seven Steps of Assignment Writing discussed earlier in this chapter. You will need to allocate sufficient time to go through each of these steps carefully. Additionally, some steps—such as proofreading—are best done at a different time than other steps in the writing process (we will discuss why later).

Of course, the amount of time needed to complete each of the Seven Steps of Assignment Writing will vary based on the length and complexity of a given assignment. For instance, most students probably think that Assignment 1 would take less time to write than Assignment 2. This is likely the case if you already know what personal and client experiences you want to write about. If not, you will need to leave enough time to reflect upon those experiences.

Here are a few tips on good time management:

- Once you have an outline, identify where you need to do outside research and realistically estimate how much time this will take in hours.
- Estimate how much time (again, in hours) it will take you to write a rough draft of your assignment.
- Estimate how much time it will take you to proofread your assignment and ensure that it contains all the required elements. We strongly recommend that you do not write and proofread your assignment at the same time.
- Estimate how much time it will take you to format the paper correctly (including APA 7th Edition in-text and reference citations, title pages, abstract, etc.).
- Many schools have writing centers—freely available and established resources where students can seek help with all aspects of the writing process. We recommend that you look into using these services and consider how much time you should allow for appointments, etc. These services can be used in conjunction with this handbook to improve all aspects of your writing.
- Working backwards from the due date, and with a calendar by your side, block out time to work on your assignment. We recommend scheduling this time on your work-dedicated electronic calendar, so your time doesn't get taken up with more pressing issues like work, family time, or a beer with your buddies. You now have a work plan that, hopefully, you can live with!

Writing Exercise 1.3 is an example of how you can create a schedule that allows for each section on your outline to be completed on time. One extra tip: be generous in estimating your time for writing tasks. Often writing takes more time than you think it will.

Writing Exercise 1.3

Use the outline you created in Exercise 1.2 and estimate the time it will take you to do each of the following tasks related to this assignment prior to its due date: do research; write a complete rough draft; proofread your paper; and format your paper.

Consider your due date and your own personal schedule. Create a detailed schedule for completing the work. For example:

9/7: Finalize topic.

9/12—1-3 pm: Research the topic.

9/13—2-4 pm: Continue research.

9/19—1-3 pm: Begin drafting paper

9/20—2-4 pm: Continue drawing paper.

9/21—2-3 pm: First proofread.

9/22—10-11 am: Proofread again.

9/23—1-3 pm: Make revisions based on proofreads.

9/24—2-4 pm Continue rewriting and finalize formatting.

9/25: Submit assignment.

Be sure to set reminders or post your schedule in a place where you will see it.Important: Your schedule needs to make sense for you and should be as realistic as possible, with a little extra time worked in to cover any "just in case" scenarios.

There are tools to help with assignment organization in Chapter 6 of this handbook.

Step 3: Use scholarship for discovery and to support your ideas

Most papers in your social work program will require a certain number of outside references. In some cases, you will need to use assigned readings; in other cases, you will have to do some searching for works yourself. In this section, we will help you identify what "counts" as works of scholarship and where to find them, and suggest how you can prepare to cite these works in your final paper.

What Counts as Scholarship?

Peer-reviewed articles published in professional journals are the most rigorous forms of scholarship. In these cases, a panel of qualified reviewers—who are blind to the identities of the authors—read, review, and rate each article when it is submitted for publication. The journal editor evaluates the feedback from the reviewers and makes recommendations for editing, if warranted; they can also reject articles that fail to meet the journal's standards for good scholarship or for appropriateness for the journal.

In addition to peer-reviewed articles, books and reports are often acceptable sources to cite; however, since these are not blindly reviewed, they are not considered the "gold standard." Therefore, it is important to consider the following:

- Are books published by reputable publishers? Self-published books or those produced by politically affiliated publishing houses are not the best resources.
- Are reports produced by reputable organizations? Government agencies are reputable organizations. Private organizations using data produced by government agencies are generally considered to be reputable. Still, you should be aware of the missions of private organizations and look out for possible biases in their analysis and conclusions.

In general, items in the popular press are not considered scholarly, even though they may be published by reputable organizations. This means that an article found, for instance, in *The New York Times* would not meet the criteria for a work of scholarship and should not be used. Similarly, websites such as Wikipedia are not considered good sources of scholarship.

Where Can I Find Scholarly Material?

First, make use of your university's library! Most schools have access to numerous electronic databases that will enable you to find and access peer-reviewed articles. Many schools have librarians ready to assist you in locating material for your assignments. Note that the databases you use may differ depending on the assignment. For example, in Assignment 1, you would likely search databases related to social work practice (e.g., Social Work Abstracts or PsychINFO); while in Assignment 2, you might be more interested in searching databases with a legal basis (e.g., Nexis Uni) or that carry a wide variety of policy-related articles (e.g., EBSCO).

You may be aware of journals that have scholarly articles that could be useful to you. For example, if you read an article for your class reading assignments, the journal that published that article might generally be helpful to you for future assignments.

In addition, Google Scholar is a useful tool for identifying works of scholarship that you might not have found through your school's databases. You can configure Google Scholar to highlight articles that are freely available by entering your library information. To do this, do the following:

- Access Google Scholar at https://scholar.google.com/.
- Use the dropdown menu to go to Settings.
- Select Library Links, enter the name of your school and then press Save. Future searches will highlight articles available to you in search results. Simply click the link provided, use your school's sign-in credentials, as needed, and you've got it!

One final source of scholarship is the bibliographies in your textbooks, required readings, and other scholarly material. Since the authors of articles build upon knowledge produced by others, you may be able to use resources that are listed in their reference sections.

Finally, your school may have printed journals in the library and your librarian can help you identify which may fit best with your work. In all cases, whether you are using electronic or printed sources, it is always best to use ones that are relatively recent. An article from 1980 is likely to be less informative about the current situation than one written in the last five years or so. While this is not always true, it stands to reason that the publication date is an important factor to consider.

Reading the Material

Once you find the material you wish to use for your assignments, you will need to read it carefully. Suggestions for critical reading, thinking, and notetaking can be found in Chapter 7.

Get Ready to Cite by Taking Notes

Any idea that is not your own must be cited. As you read and prepare to write your paper, take notes and be sure to keep track of the sources of your ideas. One way to do this is to make a notation of your sources as you prepare the outline for your paper. Another way is to use index cards to write notes, with one card being used for each source and idea. When you are ready to write, you can group cards with the same topic together.

When citing ideas that are not your own, you need to differentiate between direct quotes and summaries. To avoid making an error in your final paper, we recommend putting quotation marks around your notes if the material is taken word for word from the source. When doing so, be sure to note the page or paragraph number in which the material is found, as you will need this later. Paragraph numbers are used when page numbers are not available, as in many online publications. If you can summarize what you have read, which is usually preferred by instructors, you will still need to note the source of the material; however, you will not need the exact page number. It is a good idea to keep track of page or paragraph numbers even when you are summarizing ideas, in case you need to reread the original work later. Additional information about citing ideas from published articles can be found in Chapter 5 of this book and in the APA *Publication Manual, Seventh Edition*.

Writing Exercise 1.4

Identify sources of scholarship that will help you complete your written assignment. Then, do one of the following:

- If you have a writing partner, share your strategy for searching for scholarly materials. For example, what specific databases or journals may help you meet the requirements of this assignment? Since you are both working on the same assignment, you will likely be able to help each other identify databases or journals that could be useful to you both.
- If you are working on your own, devise a plan to search for the scholarship you will need to complete your assignment. If you need help, ask a classmate, see your instructor, and/or ask a librarian for assistance.

Writing Exercise 1.5

- Use your outline and identify the material needed to complete your assignment. Then read and take notes.
- Summarize the main points, particularly those most relevant to your assignment. This will make writing your paper easier later on.

Step 4: Write a Rough Draft

Once you have well-developed outline for your paper and the notes to address the scholarship necessary to support your work, it is time to begin writing. Most good writers work through a series of drafts. Typically, students do not have a huge amount of time to write each paper, so we suggest two drafts: the first draft and the final draft. How you write is up to you, but it is a good idea to set aside blocks of time to work on your drafts. Some people find it helpful to write each section of the paper by following the order of the outline, while others tackle the easiest sections first. No matter how you choose to write your paper, here are some helpful hints that have worked well for us and our students in the past:

- Refer to your outline frequently. You might want to keep it open on your computer or have a hard copy at hand to refer to throughout your writing session.
- Use headings. Major sections of your paper, like those identified in your outline, should have headings. These will help guide the reader through your paper section by section. If sections are long, you might want to include subheadings as well. An illustration of headings and subheadings can be found in Chapter 5 of this book.
- Write in "chunks." To keep your train of thought going, try to write at least an entire section (or subsection, if the section is very long) in one session.
- Make sure everything in your outline is covered in your draft in the order set out in your outline. This will help ensure logical thought progression in your final paper.

- Consider writing introductions and conclusions last. You might want to include some details from the body of your paper in these sections. We have found that it is often easier to write these after the remainder of the paper has been drafted.
- If an idea is not your own, cite it immediately in your draft. If you are using a direct quote from an author or summarizing someone else's ideas, include a citation. In your first draft, you can include your citations or write "(PUT CITATION HERE)" as a placeholder. This way, you will not forget to include it later.

Writing Exercise 1.6

Write the rough draft of your assignment; then do the following:

- If you have a writing partner, share your draft with them. Do they think you have met all the requirements of the assignment? Do they have suggestions for improving your paper? If so, make note of these and consider revising your paper based on their recommendations.
- If you are working on your own, wait as long you can (we recommend one day if possible) to let your brain rest and allow you to review your draft with "fresh eyes." Compare your draft to your outline. If there is something missing, fill it in. If you have gathered additional material that is not covered in your outline, consider whether you need it to meet the requirements of this assignment. If not, do not include it. You might want to save it for a future paper. Or you may want to delete it.

Step 5: Format Your Paper

Once you have a decent first draft of your paper, you will need to ensure it is formatted properly. At the very least, you will need correctly formatted citations in the text of your paper and in your reference page. Some instructors may also require an abstract and/or a title page. An abstract is a brief summary of your paper, usually limited to between 100 and 150 words. It is placed after the title page and before the beginning of your paper. The reference page, entitled "References," includes all cited resources formatted according to the reference style in APA 7th Edition. Be sure to understand what your instructor requires before submitting your paper. More on APA 7th Edition writing style, including examples from commonly used sources, can be found in Chapter 5.

Step 6: Proofread Before You Submit!

Proofread your final paper at least twice, but ideally three times. Most writers—even those who are experienced—make mistakes. Writing requires concentration; attention to the details of grammar and spelling may initially be ignored while you are in the process of expressing and organizing your ideas; however, they will need to be addressed before you submit your final draft. In our experience, students who proofread get higher grades.

As noted above, it is helpful to take a break from the writing process before beginning to proofread, as a pause will help you clear your head and look at your work with fresh eyes when you return to it. This will make the proofreading process much more effective.

Here are some tips for successful proofreading:

- When reading your paper for editing purposes, we strongly suggest you read it out loud. Be sure to read only what is written and not what you think is written. Hearing what you wrote improves the editing process immensely!
- Plan to read through your paper at least twice, but ideally three times. The first time through, consider the content. Are you communicating what you want to say in the best way you know how? For example, if you were your instructor reading this assignment for the first time, would they fully grasp the messages you are trying to share? Does this meet the requirements of the assignment? If all requirements are not met, you might need to reword some sections, edit them, or move them around to improve the logical flow of your paper. This first proofread will take the longest, so allow adequate time for a thorough review and revision.
- When you read your paper through the second time, look for grammatical or punctuation errors that you might have missed previously. Pay attention to errors that your word-processing software points out. Do you need to add a comma or change the

spelling of words? Are there typos or citation errors? Refer to Chapter 4 to review common writing problems if you are unsure.

• If possible, ask someone else to read your paper. Then ask them to state the main points that you have communicated. Did this meet the goal of your assignment? If not, you might need to edit your paper further.

• If your instructor has provided you with a grading rubric, now is the time to review it. Try grading your own assignment based on what you have written. If you are not satisfied with your grade, look for weaknesses and revise accordingly.

While this may seem like a long list of proofreading activities, it is likely that this process will take you a relatively short amount of time if you have carefully followed the other steps in the writing process.

As you complete the proofreading process and make changes to your paper, you are continually improving your draft. You may want to use software to assist you in weeding out grammatical and spelling errors; but for content, you are on your own. Reading your paper at least twice for content is an important step toward writing success.

Writing Exercise 1.7

Proofread your paper thoroughly, editing the paper as you go. Then do the following:

• If you have a writing partner, exchange papers with them and read each other's assignments. Provide detailed feedback for each other, with suggestions for improving the writing. Give each other grades for the assignment using a grading rubric, if one has been provided for you.

• If you are working on your own, proofread your paper, making edits as you go. As you work through this process, be sure to read your paper aloud, as this will make a big difference to the quality of your editing! If you have access to a writing center, you may want to bring in your final draft for a review before submitting it.

Step 7: Submitting your Assignment

After all that work, it is finally time to submit your paper. Based on our experience, here are some helpful tips to ensure this step goes smoothly:

- Make careful note of the due date for the assignment. It is always best to submit assignments on time. Instructors often reduce grades for late assignments.
- If you have to use TurnItIn or some other plagiarism detection software, read the report that results from your submission. A good score does not guarantee that you have not committed a plagiarism offense. Low scores only indicate that there is not much that is worrisome. Look at everything highlighted and make sure that you have cited properly throughout. In short, use these tools to help you and not simply to provide evidence that you have not plagiarized. If things are highlighted that seem to need citations, do a final edit before submitting your assignment. If you are unsure of how best to use TurnItIn or other software, ask your instructor or your school's writing center staff for help.
- Do not plan on submitting your work at the last minute. If you submit your work through a learning management system such as Canvas or Blackboard, be aware that technical glitches can sometimes interrupt that process. These can include software upgrades or faulty internet connections. If you turn in hard copies of your assignments, glitches such as broken printers can also occur. Plan for these eventualities. They happen more frequently than you might imagine.

Once you have submitted your paper, pat yourself on the back for a job well done! When you receive feedback, be sure to read through your instructor's comments and heed their advice in the preparation of future assignments.

CONCLUSION

Written assignments are still the primary method for evaluating students in social work programs. Additionally, well-written assignments pave the way for good professional communications, now and in the future. Using a structured method for writing, such as that described in detail in this chapter, helps you demonstrate your social work competence throughout your academic career.

Quick Tips: Writing Checklist

- Read your assignments carefully to assure you understand what is required.
- Write an outline based on the requirements of the assignment.
- Research your topic using scholarly sources.
- Credit your sources as you research, making notes on direct quotes and summarized content.
- Use the headings and subheadings of your outline to organize the text of your paper.
- Proofread, proofread, proofread before you submit your completed assignment.

WRITING FOR THE FIELD

Write Like a Professional Social Worker

INTRODUCTION

In this chapter, we address writing skills for a successful internship experience. This chapter is not meant to replace your program's internship manual. Instead, it aims to assist you with the writing tasks found on most internship placements. We provide a step-by-step approach with examples of writing for social work practice in both micro and macro settings.

Before we delve into work on writing skills, let's look at the various areas of professional social work practice. The National Association of Social Work (NASW) lists the following areas of practice:

- Administration and Management;
- Advocacy and Community Organizing;
- Aging;
- Developmental Disabilities;
- Healthcare;
- Justice and Corrections;
- Mental Health and Clinical Social Work;
- Mental Health and Substance Abuse Social Work;
- Occupation and Employee Assistance;
- International Social Work;
- Policy and Planning;
- Politics;
- Public Welfare;
- Research; and
- School Social Work.

DOI: 10.4324/9781003168713-3

While it is possible for social work students to be assigned an internship placement in any of these areas, it is more likely you will be asked to select your preferences from a shorter list of available areas supported by your program and local agencies. Let's walk through the writing skills you may need to develop on your internship placement. We begin by examining the technical aspects of your field of practice.

TECHNICAL ASPECTS OF FIELDS OF PRACTICE

Different fields of practice have different technical aspects based on the unique tasks involved in serving their respective clients. For example, social workers in a healthcare setting need different knowledge and skills than social workers in a school setting. Although this may seem obvious, it is a distinction that requires different writing skills to support the different tasks. Students are expected to use the technical terms that are appropriate to the setting. This may mean you are expected to learn a new vocabulary and use it when writing reports, filling out forms, and writing chart notes. Here are steps to follow that can assist in the learning process:

- **Step 1:** Make time to read about your internship's field of practice. There are several ways to jump right into the technical terms you will need to know through reading. First, search the internet for information, ideas, and current issues that you expect to need in your work. If you are not just starting out, move on to more complex terms that are coming your way. Be sure to relate what you have found to social work practice. For example, if you are reading about medications, ask yourself how you would apply this knowledge to working with individuals and families. If you are reading about a new law or social policy, how would this apply to your macro assignment?

- **Step 2:** After you become involved in the learning process, keep a notebook or a dedicated file on your computer in which you can write out new terms—taking care to use the correct spellings, pronunciations, and definitions—and details of how to use them in your social work role. Some technical terms have several variations, such as medications, diagnoses, and diagnostic tests. Examples include prefaces such as "hyper-" and "hypo-," or "inter-" and "intra-." Be sure to learn the differences because you may need to refer to them in your writing. For macro practices, keep up to date with the latest strategies that may affect your community, including new government proposals and judicial rulings.

- **Step 3:** If you don't know a technical term, first try looking it up on the internet. If you need more clarity, ask your internship instructor for help. There may be subtleties in practice or new methods of treatment at your internship site that you will not find in the public literature. Although this chapter focuses on writing, speaking to clients and consumers about technical terms calls for knowing the correct pronunciation. Your internship instructor can help you with writing and speaking about important terms and concepts related to your internship field of practice. Commonly used abbreviations and technical terms can be found in Appendix B.

WRITING IN OFFICIAL DOCUMENTS: CASE NOTES AND LOGS

Case notes and organization activity logs are legal documents that demonstrate agency work. Case notes for practice with clients can be used as evidence in court cases in a variety of contexts. Examples include child custody and employment discrimination cases. Case notes can also be used by state and federal audits as evidence for agency reimbursements from insurance providers and proof of a variety of issues, such as a parent's competency to care for her child or a client's ability to return to work. In legal cases, case notes can confirm suspected fraud, malpractice, and child custody decisions, to name just a few. As an intern, your agency's educational instructor will read and sign off on your case notes; when you graduate, you may be on your own. Activities notes—sometimes called logs—used by community organization agencies are similar, in that they can be called up by auditors for documentation of an organization's progress. The best way to manage documentation is to focus on the goals and objectives in your treatment/activities plans and utilize facts as evidence to document progress. Knowing the potential importance of these documents, your choice of words and use of a professional tone can enhance their value. When in doubt, ask for guidance from your internship instructor. Here are some tips on case and log note writing:

- **Case notes:** As with all social work practice with clients, it is important to separate facts from interpretations. Facts are what you observe (hear and see); interpretations are the meanings that can be culled from what you hear and see based upon your observations. In other words, facts are to be written first, followed by interpretations based on facts. For example, you may write: "Mrs. Jones was tearful throughout the session. I asked her how she felt, and she replied, 'Sad and angry.'" You may suspect she was depressed, but you have no documented evidence of this at this time. You can interpret her tearfulness and her words "sad and angry" by writing: "It appears that Mrs. Jones may be experiencing a bout of depression, but additional evidence is needed to confirm." Alternatively, you may forgo the idea that she may be depressed until a future session. When you learn more about Mrs. Jones' feelings, you can use the phrase "as evidenced by" as a way of documenting your interpretation. You may want to express views that are not fully evidenced to your internship instructor or in team meetings. Corroboration may encourage you to seek more information from your client but should not be used as your evidence. Do not write, "Dr. Smith also thinks Mrs. Jones is depressed."

- Case notes on groups differ from those on individuals in that you are writing about numerous interactions among group members. Since group work is assessed by the processes occurring in each session, case notes can reflect on both the content and the effects of group discussions, both on the group as a whole and on individual members. Assessing processes requires an awareness of the group's goals and objectives, as well as its structure, member concerns, leadership, and agency climate. Groups that are called "open door" allow new members to join, and some members to leave and come back, either as assigned by the agency or at will with the permission of the group. Closed groups for the most part keep a steady membership census where membership is based upon characteristics of individuals. In either case, notes typically monitor the progress and processes of the entire group in achieving goals. Group members who are silent or rarely contribute are denoted, as they may be a poor fit for the group and may require individualized counseling. For insurance reimbursements, some agencies require a short progress note on each member after the group meeting—usually once a week.

- **Log activity notes:** These can be used to describe events, policy projects, and activities related to the agency's missions in the community or organization to which they serve. Logs are written for agencies and social service organizations to demonstrate their work and accomplishments to the public and to funders. Social work interns assigned to government-sponsored community activist organizations, such as a city's civic development agency, may be asked to contribute to a log at regular time intervals or after specially organized events. The same may be true for students working in nonprofit social service work and in some religious-based fundraising organizations. Most of the guidelines for writing case notes are also applicable to logs. There may be differences based on the internship site's mission and even its history. You should always check with your internship instructor for important details if you are asked to contribute log notes.

- **Identifying others:** Clients and professionals should be addressed by their formal names and titles in agency writing. You may be on a first-name basis with agency clients and staff when speaking, but this should not be followed through in written records that are formal documents. Your internship instructor and possibly your professor in your practice class will advise you on professional titles, using prefixes such as "Dr." or suffixes such as "MD" or "DO." For information on non-professional pronouns, consult the section on bias-free writing in Chapter 5 in this book—or simply ask people how they prefer to be addressed. One important point: when identifying clients, be consistent in how you refer to them. If you are working with Mrs. Gray and identify her as such in your first note, continue to refer to her as "Mrs. Gray" in every note that follows. Changing a name or even a pronoun— such as sometimes writing "Ms. Gray"—can confuse readers who may be referring to your notes long after you have left the agency.

- **Identifying yourself:** How you write your name on documents as your signature is another issue that can be decided at the very beginning of your internship. In most internship sites, you will write your first and last name, followed by the words "Social Work Intern." An example would be: "Jane Green, Social Work Intern." Some agencies may prefer "John Green, Social Work Student Intern." Still others may ask you to include the initials of the social work program you are attending, such as: "Jess Green, Social Work Intern, [your school's initials]." In any case, be consistent in using your signature so you may be identified even years later by administrators or clinicians. When in doubt, ask your internship instructor for directions.

- **Pronouns:** Avoid using pronouns such as "I", "we," or "our" whenever possible. It is best to keep your writing in the third person, using descriptive language. Instead of writing, "Our agency's rules state …," write "The agency's rules state …" Instead of, "We were off last Tuesday," write "The staff had the day off last Tuesday."

- **Attributions:** Use attributions only when necessary. Let other professionals write their own notes. Keep your notes focused on your work. It is not necessary to write about what another staff member stated directly to you or said in the team meeting. If the agency administrator mentioned a change in agency policy, keep it out of your notes until the change is official. If the doctor told you a client's prescription is changing, don't write it down until the change has been made and the client has been informed. Exceptions may occur on occasion, such as when a staff member asks you to give directions to a client. Here is an example of when an attribution also requires use of the pronouns "me" and "I": "Dir. Jones asked me to remind Ms. Smith to call him on Wednesday and I did so."

- **Disagreements:** Keep disagreements or conflicts out of case notes and logs. For example, the staff doctor is discharging your client and you disagree, thinking she needs another week in the facility; or the agency is cutting down its evening hours and you know this will inconvenience several of your clients and may cause them to stop their group therapy sessions. While these are legitimate concerns, voice them directly to the appropriate people. Disagreements with staff, colleagues, internship instructors, supervisors, or professors are not to be written in agency notes. Your notes may be read by people not directly working at your internship site, such as auditors or lawyers; or later by new social work interns and other staff members. Writing about disagreements can raise questions about the agency's efficacy and your professional comportment after disagreements have been resolved—even years later, when you have moved on.

- **Making changes:** Case notes and logs are not easily changed. With modern electronic records and paper charts, there are procedures to follow when correcting an entry mistake. If this occurs, first ask your internship instructor if you need to make changes and, if so, how to edit or change the original records. Once you have your internship instructor's agreement to change a note, follow the specified procedure. Instructions on changing an incorrect case note can vary depending on the use of electronic platforms or paper formats. When working with electronic note systems, do not assume your former experience with note changes at another internship site will also apply where you are now. Electronic platforms often differ regarding corrections, so it is important to obtain specific directions and possibly assistance from an experienced staff member before you proceed. There are also rules on making changes in paper charts and logs. Find out what they are before you begin. In general, crossing out the incorrect word or phrase followed by the change and your initials is the required procedure. Still, ask for directions; as an example of your need to find out the specifics, some agencies require the use of black ink only. The use of chemical whiteouts is also prohibited by most agencies.

Documentation of cases or organization activities is a professional social work task. Depending on whether you are a fourth-year bachelor of social work student or a master of social work (MSW) student, you will be asked to document your work at your internship site. All social work staff, students, MSW graduates, and internship instructors are expected to adhere to agency procedures for writing in charts and logs.

Exercise 2.1

Select a case or log scenario from your practice textbook and, with a writing partner, write a case or log note.
- Read and comment on each other's work. What looks good? Where is there room for improvement?
- If working alone, share your note with your internship supervisor and ask for feedback.

TECHNOLOGY AND WRITING FOR YOUR INTERNSHIP

There is so much information about the use of technology in internship practice in social work available today. You can start by exploring the resources at the end of this chapter. NASW, the Council on Social Work Education, the Association of Social Work Boards, and the Clinical Social Work Association have jointly published a guide entitled *Technology in Social Work Practice*. This publication spells out the ethical requirements that social workers need to follow when communicating electronically. Please refer to it for guidance on how to use technology in practice. It is also a good idea to download the guide and others like it onto your computer for future reference, as many are written for all social workers, not specifically for students.

PROCESS RECORDINGS AND JOURNALS

Process recordings differ from case notes and logs in an important way. Unlike case notes and activity logs, process recordings and journals are educational tools that belong to students and are used for learning purposes and supervision. Their function is to demonstrate your work with clients. They also allow you to express your ideas related to your work, including suggestions on how to improve.

Internship instructors and professors read process recordings and journals to assess your work and provide helpful feedback on your achievements as well as suggestions to improve your interventions. There are a variety of process recordings and journal templates, although the latter are sometimes offered to students as less formalized outlines. Both may begin with a review of a social work student-client session with goals and objectives. As a quick review, goals are the planned outcome of the social work intervention; objectives are specific measurable steps to achieve the targeted goal. For example, a goal may be for the client to gain insight into their behavior toward their parents. An objective to measure the goal might be identifying ways to improve and monitoring progress in improving family communication.

Some templates for process recordings may require a narrative of the direct words spoken by you and your client for the entire session. Others may ask you to select the most important sections of the session to describe either in exact words or by paraphrasing.

Most call for short memos related to students' critical reflections and feelings about the session, with suggestions for improved or alternative ways of addressing the client and situation. Written progress notes are typical; although there are some models that exclusively use voice recordings or videos, and some that combine written work with other media. Your professor will instruct you on the type of process recording to use in your internship setting.

It is unusual, but if you face conflicting instructions on writing process recordings from your practice professor and your internship instructor, speak with your professor to resolve the matter. If there are differences, it is for the school and the agency to work out a solution between them. Your task is to use process recordings as part of your educational learning experience.

Here are examples of process recording instructions and templates.

Student Name:
Internship Instructor Name:
Interview Date and Session Number:
Indicate the Phase of Treatment (i.e., engagement, assessment, intervention, termination):

Generalist Year Chart

Content of Contact	Student's Feelings	Student's Assessment	Internship Instructor Comments
	Record what you felt as the dialog was taking place.	Analyze skills, interactions and theory used during the dialog.	Comments on strengths and areas for improvement.
Interaction 1:			
Interaction 2:			
Interaction 3:			
Interaction 4:			
Interaction 5:			
Interaction 6:			
Interaction 7:			
Interaction 8:			
Interaction 9:			

Description of Contact (i.e., client demographics—please do not include client identifying information—presenting problem, interview location, or another present during the interview):

Purpose of the Session (interview/observation):

Goals for the Session (the outcomes you hope to achieve):

Assessment and Self-reflection

Goals and Objectives: Did you meet your goals for the session? What did you do well? What would you do differently in the future?

Accomplishments and Plans: What is your observation of the client's strengths and areas of difficulty? What has been accomplished in the current session, and what are your plans for the next sessions?

Questions for Supervision: Areas to include in your internship instructor conference. Include issues of oppression and diversity, value and ethical dilemmas, countertransference, etc.

⋆ Adapted from West Chester University Social Work Department and Montclair State University Department of Social Work and Child Advocacy

---

Student Name:

Internship Instructor Name:

Interview Date and Session Number:

Indicate the Phase of Treatment (i.e., engagement, assessment, intervention, termination):

Description of Contact (i.e., client demographics—please do not include client identifying information—presenting problem, interview location, other present during interview):

Purpose of the Session (interview/observation):

Goals for the Session (the outcomes you hope to achieve):

Assessment and Self-Reflection

Goals and Objectives: Did you meet your goals? What did you do well? What would you do differently in the future?

Accomplishments and Plans: What is your observation of the client's strengths and areas of difficulty? What has been accomplished in the current session, and what are your plans for the next sessions?

Specialization Year Chart

	Student's Feelings	Student's Assessment	Internship Instructor Comments
Record word-for-word dialog of the most significant part of the interaction between the student and the client.	Record what you felt as the dialog was taking place.	Analyze skills, interactions and theory used during the dialog.	Comments on strengths and areas for improvement.
Interaction 1:			
Interaction 2:			
Interaction 3:			
Interaction 4:			
Interaction 5:			
Interaction 6:			
Interaction 7:			
Interaction 8:			
Interaction 9:			

Questions for Supervision: Areas to include in your internship instructor conference. Include issues of oppression and diversity, value and ethical dilemmas, countertransference, etc.

★Adapted from West Chester University Social Work Department and Montclair State University, Department of Social Work and Child Advocacy

Journals are useful in most internship settings and are most often prominent in internships that involve work with macro systems. These include, but are not limited to, work in organizational activist work, fundraising, policy, and community service interventions. They are helpful in organizing your thoughts and reflecting on both formal and informal agency meetings and activities. Here is an example of a journal recording template.

Section I: Project/Activity Description

Student Name:

Internship Instructor Name:

Activity/Project Description: Discuss the background for the activity and include relevant context.

Date of Activity/Project:

Goals/Objectives for the Activity/Project:

MSW Journal Recording Column Chart

Description	Obstacles	Assessment of Activity	Student's Feelings	Internship Instructor Comments
Discuss the purpose of the activity/ project and the need being addressed. Include the primary steps needed to complete the activity/project and list the steps in chronological order (if relevant). Include projected completion dates and internal and external resources needed to complete the activity/project (if relevant).	Discuss your initial thoughts about the potential problems/ challenges related to the activity/ project described.	Explore questions raised during the process of completing the activity/ project. Include a retrospective evaluation of your own performance and discuss how tasks may have been done differently.	Record what you felt during the activity/ project described.	

Assessment and Self-Reflection

Assessment and Self-Reflection: Did you meet your goals? What did you do well? What would you do differently in the future?

Accomplishments and Plans: What has been accomplished in the current interaction? What are the next steps, in your opinion?

Questions for Supervision: Areas to include in your internship instructor conference. Include issues of oppression and diversity, value and ethical dilemmas, countertransference, etc.
⋆ Adapted from Montclair State University Department of Social Work and Child Advocacy.

For an additional example of how journals are used by internship students, refer to the journal sample provided by Western Michigan University for its students at https://wmich.edu/sites/default/files/attachments/u57/2013/appendix-g-2-sample-field-log-journal-entries.pdf.

CLIENT ASSESSMENTS, REFERRALS, AND REPORTS

An important part of professional social work involves writing client assessments, referrals, and reports. Many internship sites use electronic templates, although you may find that paper forms are provided in your internship. Assessments, referrals, and reports may be written by student interns, usually with oversight from internship instructors. Although they do not typically attract the same scrutiny as case notes and internship logs, they can be included in court proceedings in rare cases. They often can be significant in the outcome of client placements and ultimately, in goal achievement.

Assessments

Assessments of clients are typically conducted upon entry into a health or behavioral health facility or social work agency. Professional referrals to an agency may come with a detailed written assessment from the referring organization. Upon accepting a new client, most social work departments or agencies will conduct their own intake assessment that requires documentation. Social workers are often asked to complete this documentation or, alternatively, contribute to sections that are focused on the social services the agency offers. As a student intern, you may be asked to participate in the intake process, which includes the interview and the written assessment document.

For students working in macro settings—such as administrative, community, or policy settings—assessments may be used when taking on a new project. Here too, there may be interviews with project stakeholders that require a written report as part of an assessment. It is likely that social work interns in macro-systems internship education sites will be involved in these processes.

In all intake assessments, it is important to complete the intake form in full, leaving no blank or unanswered questions. A non-response could be interpreted as a failure to see the question or unwillingness to offer an answer. If you do not know the answer to a question on the form, you can write responses such as "not known," or "not available" ("NA"). There may be additional notations suggested by your agency that can be used when information cannot be provided. When in doubt, check with your internship instructor.

Referrals

Social workers are often asked to refer clients to other services, either in lieu of or in addition to the current service. When referring a client to a large service facility or a city or state agency, it is likely they will have their own electronic forms. For these referrals, similar to intake forms, it is important to respond to all questions within the space provided. If you need more space, you can often add additional pages. Again, if you do not know the answer to a question on the form, do not leave it blank—write "NA" (not available); or if there is a code for "NA," use the code. In most cases, you will need to provide only the information asked for; but if you feel strongly that there is additional information the referral agency staff should know, you can usually add it at the end. It is a good idea to consult your internship instructor before making additions to referral forms, as this may affect the client's chances of being accepted by the referral facility. For both electronic and paper referral forms, you may either make corrections or choose to discard the form with mistakes and start over with a fresh copy.

Not all referral forms require as much detail as the example above. Sometimes, you may be able to refer a client by phone or video conference and then fill out a shorter form. As with all your written work for your internship, a case note should follow.

Most community referrals ask for fewer details. Macro-systems social work interns typically will add a phone call or video conference to the referral process. Nevertheless, a written form is almost always required. A typical community agency referral can be found at the end of this chapter. Written reports are more common in macro-systems work in communities and organizations, where social work interns are often required to report on projects. These reports can be for internal agency use or may be part of a larger report for external auditors or funders. An inclusive guide to social work report writing can be found at the end of this chapter. Keep in mind that organizations may have useful templates for reports. Ask your internship instructor if your organization has a format they expect reports to follow. Alternatively, you may want to ask to see previously written reports used by your agency with a similar subject to that on which you have been asked to write. Sample reports can give you ideas on page length, organizing content, and the overall tone that is expected.

Exercise 2.2

With a partner or by yourself, find referral forms on the internet that are suitable to your internship site:

- Using scenarios from your practice textbook and the referral form, refer a client to:
  1 a mental health agency close to their home;
  2 supervised housing; and
  3 another scenario of your choice.
- If your site is a community agency or social work macro organization, refer a client to an appropriate setting according to their needs.
- Share your work with your internship partner or, if working alone, with your internship supervisor.

WRITING DIFFERENCES BASED ON FIELDS OF PRACTICE

Throughout this chapter, we have referred to writing expectations based on differing internship assignments (see the 15 areas of practice noted by the NASW at the beginning of this chapter). Regardless of internship site, student learning in internships is typically divided into three methods—working with:

- individuals and families;
- groups; and
- communities and organizations.

Depending on your practice context, within these methods are unique categories and populations, as well as related social policies. For the most part, these differences will not affect process recordings or internship notes; however, there may be some important differences. We begin this section with a discussion of differences between individuals, couples, and families; and then move on to groups, communities, and organizations. Keep in mind that the following examples are brief illustrations. For more detailed information, you may wish to consult specialized guides to your internship placement category, some of which are included at the end of this chapter.

Individuals, Couples, and Families

Although individuals, couples, and families are usually combined in social work practice assignments, they require a different set of knowledge and skills. The process recording for individuals may largely speak to the client's relationships and supports in their environment, as well as their relationship with you. When working with couples and families, the focus is on the relationships within these groups, with limited references to your interventions. In couples and family sessions, how individuals relate to each other is demonstrated by their words, facial expressions, body language, and overall comportment; whereas in individual sessions, outside-of-session relationships are limited to the descriptions the client presents. In both types of sessions, the process is important; but the focus of attention differs and should be reflected in your process recording and chart writing.

Here is an example of a chart note written about an individual client. Instead of going to his high-school classes, Roberto spends time at the local car repair shop. You write:

> *Roberto stated he sometimes doesn't go to classes and instead spends time at the local car repair shop. When asked why he makes this choice,*

he looked away without providing an answer. Further investigation is needed to understand why he did not provide an answer.

If Roberto's family is your client, you might write the note differently:

Having been made aware that Roberto spends time at the local car repair shop on many school days, the Rios family members—both parents and younger sister Benita—and Roberto were asked to express their feelings about his decision to cut classes. Neither Benita nor Roberto responded. Mrs. Rios shook her head and stated she did not understand what Roberto hoped to accomplish. Mr. Rios looked away and grimaced. It seemed that the family were previously unaware of this, although it is not clear that this pertained to Benita. The news of Roberto's actions seemed to split the family, with parents on one side showing dismay and anger, and the children on the other side adopting a "So what?" attitude. These dynamics need further examination.

Your internship instructor will guide you with your focus and how to move forward.

Groups

When working with groups, social work student interns have the unique challenge of focusing on the group process and assessing individual members as they participate in the group. The group focus is determined by the stated group goals, group membership, structure, agency rules, and the intersectionality of external events and internal member relations. While the details of specific groups vary, the overall strategy for writing process recordings or case notes is to focus on the group process rather than the words of individual members. The general rule is that phrases like, "The group decided …" or "Group members agreed to …" are preferable to "John stated …" Of course, you should defer to your internship instructor's guidance on writing about groups. As noted earlier in this chapter, agencies may expect group leaders to record group member attendance or contributions as a way of documenting treatment for insurance purposes.

Community Settings

Students placed in community settings may be involved with planning, implementing, and evaluating community events such as a fundraising community breakfast or a health fair. These are simply examples, as there are multiple possibilities for organized events to benefit community members and visitors.

In terms of writing, interns document their community work in process recordings and in organizational logs that keep track of community work and events. There may also be times when interns are asked to take minutes at community meetings. Although community assignment writing usually focuses on goals, processes, and outcomes of community-based projects, at times interns may be asked to interview community stakeholders and leaders and write up summaries for agency records and newsletters. It is important to ask your internship instructor for guidance and, if possible, to provide you with examples of previously well-written work by former workers or interns.

Organizations

Organizational placements provide students with experience in a variety of social work practice areas—for example, legal, social policy, and environmental groups; nursing homes; addiction services; halfway houses for formerly incarcerated individuals; education sites; and many more. Organizations should have mission statements that articulate their overarching goals and guide their work. They may also have manuals that explicitly state their required day-to-day activities and staff obligations. Each organization also has explicit and implicit expectations for social work staff, including interns, and for clients. Because organizations differ in so many ways, the first task for interns in these settings is to learn the history and current functioning structure of their assigned sites and follow normative behavior as closely as possible. This may be as simple as learning who can be addressed by their first names and who expects you to use their titles.

Writing can also take on normative rules. There may be privacy rules to adhere to in referring to clients, family members, and staff. There may be certain words to avoid—such as "handicapped" or "addict"—that your internship instructor can bring to your attention. There may be rules related to disclosing clients' diagnoses, such as Health Insurance Portability and Accountability Act (HIPAA) rules, in written referrals. Learning the organization's culture is an ongoing assignment for social work interns as writing tasks move from beginning work to more complex tasks.

Interns placed in specialized organizations may experience writing on all three levels: individuals, couples, and families; groups; and communities. With the help of your internship instructor and practice professor, you will learn to incorporate the agency's unique mission with clients' particular needs.

CONCLUSION

With so many possible internship placements, this chapter attempts to categorize them according to their function. Your internship instructor and your practice teacher will provide you with your program's forms, and directions for writing case notes and log entries. This chapter is meant to be a supplement to accepted general guidelines and does not replace specific requirements given to you by your instructors. Some social work students may be employed in social service agencies prior to beginning their formal social work education. Working in other capacities at an agency that is now the site of your internship may call for a different set of writing skills. Our best advice is to follow the direction of your social work educators when working in your social work student capacity.

Quick Tips: Writing Checklist

- Follow the instructions your internship supervisor gives you. Since no internship site is exactly alike, there may be particular rules for writing notes or logs at your site.
- Stay up to date with technical terms used at your internship site. Keep a notebook for site-specific terms and refer to it for proper usage and spelling when writing notes.
- Back up all notes with evidence—either observable or from previous documents.
- Keep in mind that notes are legal documents and cannot be deleted or erased. They may be corrected with your internship supervisor's signature.
- Learn and follow your internship site's rules for writing and you ask for guidance as needed.

ADDITIONAL EXERCISES

- Read your program's fieldwork manual and copy information that you may not have known and that seems new to you. Ask for clarity from your practice teacher or your internship instructor.
- Read the 2021 version of the NASW Code of Ethics and copy the sections that relate to your internship work assignment. It can be found in English at https://www.socialworkers.org/About/Ethics/Code-of-Ethics/Code-of-Ethics-English and in Spanish at https://www.socialworkers.org/About/Ethics/Code-of-Ethics/Code-of-Ethics-Spanish.

FURTHER INFORMATION

References

- Forman, A. *A Guide to Social Work Field Experiences*. https://mastersinsocialworkonline.org/resources/field-placement/
- Gibson, K. & Carroll, M.J. (2023). Social work field education: Changing with the times. *Social Work Today*, 19(2) p.20. https://www.socialworktoday.com/archive/MA19p20.shtml
- Mathiyazhagan, S. (2022). Field practice, emerging technologies and human rights. The emergence of tech social workers. *Journal of Human Rights and Social Work*, 7, p.441–448.
- National Association of Social Workers. (2017). *Technology in Social Work Practice*. https://www.socialworkers.org/includes/newincludes/homepage/PRA-BRO-33617.TechStandards_FINAL_POSTING.pdf

Books

- Glassman, U. (2015). *Finding your way through fieldwork: A social work student's guide*. Sage.
- Poulin, J., Matis, S., & Witt, H. (2018). *The social work field placement*. Springer.

Online Examples of Referral Forms and Guidelines to Report Writing

- An electronic form used by the New York City Division of Homeless Services:
  https://www1.nyc.gov/assets/dhs/downloads/pdf/DHS-Institutional-Referral-Form.pdf
- A typical community referral:
  https://www1.nyc.gov/assets/dhs/downloads/pdf/DHS-Institutional-Referral-Form.pdf
- A guide to social work report writing:
  https://guide2socialwork.com/report-writing/

OTHER FORMS OF COMMUNICATION

INTRODUCTION

So far, we have discussed writing in the context of academic papers, process recordings, assessments, and clinical notes. There are times in your education and career when you will need to communicate in other formats. For example, you will likely converse with others using emails, texts, and informal chats in online meetings. When you apply for jobs, you will need to write effective cover letters to accompany resumes; and during your career, you will have to write letters to those outside of your organization. We will cover those types of communication in this chapter.

Regardless of the form of communication you are using, here are some helpful tips to remember:

- **Consider your audience:** Depending on who you are writing to, your audience may or may not include social workers. If you are not communicating with social workers or if you are not sure of people's backgrounds, avoid using jargon or terminology that is specific to the field. For example, instead of mentioning "systems theory," you could talk about "the influence of the many types of systems (e.g., schools, child welfare) that a client interacts with." In other words, express social work-specific ideas in a layperson's terms.
- **Explain who you are and why you are writing:** Unlike the formal writing that was discussed in earlier chapters (e.g., academic papers, process recordings), the types of communication discussed in this chapter are less structured. Initially, your reader

DOI: 10.4324/9781003168713-4

may not know who you are or why you are writing to them. Therefore, it is important to be clear and professional immediately as you identify yourself and the purpose of your message.

- **Be careful about how you are communicating:** If you do not know your recipient well and what their preferences are, you need to be particularly aware of the level of formality you use with them. Understand that your recipient's culture matters, and individuals from some communities prefer more formal communication than others. If in doubt, be more formal until you are instructed otherwise. This means using titles when addressing people (e.g., "Dr. X," "Ms. Social Worker").

- **Consider how your message will be perceived:** At least initially, we recommend that you keep your tone somewhat formal. We suggest avoiding emojis when emailing or texting, and not SHOUTING with capital letters. We also suggest using standard spelling, grammar, and punctuation; avoiding the use of exclamation points (!); and refraining from using acronyms such as LOL.

- **Be concise and informative:** In general, keep written communication as short as is needed in order to get your point across. This shows respect for your recipient's time by getting right to the point. If necessary, longer emails can be numbered or bulleted. Long texts are not appropriate in any situation. Additionally, you should always conclude with a comment of appreciation—something like, "Thank you for your time and consideration" is appropriate in most cases.

- **Proofread your messages:** Well-written communication is respected. Poorly written communication is not. Address this by proofreading your letter, email, or text before sending it. Preferably, this should be done by reading your communication out loud (as described in previous chapters). This will allow you to hear what your recipient is going to read. Never send any type of written communication without reading it through at least once.

EMAIL

Often, email will be your first one-on-one contact with someone. You may have an assignment due soon and want to email your professor about a question you have. Or you may be applying for a job and want to write a brief email that also includes your resume and cover letter. Regardless of your situation, emails should clearly convey what you are trying to communicate. Before sending your email, take a moment to anticipate your reader's reactions or needs.

Recently, I received the following email from a student whose name I have changed to protect their identity. The subject line contained one word—"MEET!!!":

> *Miss,*
> *I got a C- on my last paper and I didn't deserve it. Now we've got another paper do tomorrow and theres no way I can get it in on time. I'm going to fail this class if you don't give me extra credit. I don't deserve to fail. Can you meet with me later today to tell me what I can do to bring up my grade.*
> *Pat Stevens*

Poor Pat did not help herself by sending this email. Let's deconstruct what went wrong here, and then consider how this note could have been more useful to both of us. Being called "Miss" irks me (and most instructors). This is an example of the informality discussed above; the greeting should have included my last name. When in doubt, begin emails to instructors with "Dear Professor" or, more simply, "Professor …" followed by the professor's last name. Unless instructed otherwise, we strongly suggest you not use your instructor's first name in correspondence with them.

The next issue concerns the content of the email. Pat is asking to meet with me that same day to help solve her problem of possibly failing my class. This is problematic because she assumes that I will read her email as soon as she sends it, and that I can easily recall which class she is in. Pat wants me to fit her into my schedule for the same day to fix her problem. Additionally, the overall tone of the email comes across as somewhat demanding.

The final issue here is her grammar and spelling. With so many mistakes in this email, I might be inclined to think that Pat didn't really care about what she was saying or how she was saying it.

Let's consider an alternative email that could have been more effective. The revised subject line is "Meeting request re: SOWK 680 – Research Methods":

> *Dr. Z,*
>
> *I am in your SOWK 680 class on Mondays at 8am. I would like to schedule a time to meet with you. Unfortunately, your office hours do not*

OTHER FORMS OF COMMUNICATION **49**

work with my schedule. I was wondering if you would be free to meet with me on Tuesday from 5–7 pm or any time after 4 pm on Thursday?

I have been struggling in your class and I could use some assistance. I'm wondering if you could review my last paper with me to point out areas for improvement that I could apply to our assignment due next week. Also, I was also wondering if you were going to offer any extra credit opportunities this semester. I really care about school, and I want to do my best.

I look forward to hearing from you,

Pat Stevens

This email is a substantial improvement. The subject line—which I will see before opening the email—tells me what the student wants (a meeting) and which class they are in (Research Methods). The body of the email explains why the student cannot attend regular office hours; many professors will appreciate that explanation. Additionally, Pat is explaining why she wants to meet, specifying her availability, and setting out what she hopes to accomplish from the meeting. Pat's demand for extra credit has been reframed as a request. Finally, Pat has proofread her email, so it now looks and sounds professional. It is more likely that the revised email will be better received than the first version.

Writing Exercise 3.1

Working with a partner (or someone who will give you honest feedback) or on your own, construct a hypothetical email to your professor asking for an extension on your next assignment:

- Go over the six helpful hints provided at the beginning of this chapter when constructing your email.
- Proofread your email aloud. Is your request clear? Edit the text as needed.
- Proofread your email aloud AGAIN. This time, check for standard punctuation, grammar, tense, and capitalization.

- Do one of the following:
  1   If you are working with a partner, ask for feedback. Does your partner think the email could be sent out as written or do they have ideas for improving it?
  2   If you are working on your own, compare this email to ones you may have written to professors in the past. In what way(s) is your current version an improvement? Is there room for additional improvement?

TEXTS OR DIRECT MESSAGES USING MESSAGING APPS

Texts or direct messages (DMs) are the most informal and personal type of written communication we can identify. This is because the numbers or IDs associated with these are often connected to our phones or other personal accounts. Therefore, we only recommend texting or using messaging apps with people in positions of authority, such as professors or supervisors, if they have previously agreed to this or in the event of an actual emergency. If your preferred method of communication is either texting or DMs, it is perfectly acceptable to ask your professor or supervisor something like, "In the past, I've found that the easiest way to get in touch with my supervisors is through text. Would you mind if we texted each other?"

In any event, be careful when using texts or DMs with people you don't know well. These types of communication are short and often contain abbreviations, so it is easy for your message to be misinterpreted. Let's say you have permission to text your professor, and you have an emergency: you are supposed to give a presentation in an hour, but you run into terrible traffic on the way to campus. You text the following: "I'm in tons of traffic and I don't think I'm going to make it to class for my presentation." Minutes go by and you hear nothing! Now you think that the professor is mad and is ignoring you; but are they? You should be aware that in all written communication, there is often a lag in receiving a response. Despite this, you worry that your professor will be angry, so you send the following:

Source: Shutterstock/Ekaterina Chvileva)

It's difficult to know how this text will be received, and it does not add anything to your previous communication. GIFs, stickers, and emojis are best reserved for personal communications with family and friends.

As when sending an email, it is important to maintain a level of professionalism and provide context to the recipient, so they are not confused by your message. Let's consider that, instead of the message above, you send the following:

> *Hello Dr. Z. This is Melanie from your SOWK 680 class. I wanted to let you know that I will be late to class today because I am stuck in traffic. I will be there as soon as I can.*

This second message makes it clear for whom the text is intended, who you are, and the message you are hoping to convey. This is important each time you contact a professor, as they may not save your name and phone number in their contacts.

ONLINE MEETINGS

Online meeting platforms such as Zoom, Microsoft Teams, and Google Meet provide additional avenues for communication. In recent years, we have learned what works and appears professional when attending classes or other meetings online. Here is a list of "dos" for online meetings:

- **Try to find a quiet place to attend your meeting with minimal distractions:** We have seen many embarrassing situations, including one in which a significant other walked behind a student with no pants on! If you can't ensure privacy and quiet during your meeting, add a background to your account so others will not see your surroundings, and use a headset that mutes background noise whenever possible.

- **Make sure your technology is operating as it should prior to the meeting:** Check settings to ensure that your webcam and microphone are working properly before the meeting. Many platforms enable you to sign in early and test these features prior to joining the meeting.

- **Come to the meeting as if you were attending in person:** You should consider all aspects of professionalism in online meetings in the same way you would for face-to-face meetings. This means, for instance, being punctual, turning your camera on, and dressing as if you were meeting in person. If you wouldn't meet a client in pajamas, you shouldn't meet them over Zoom in pajamas either. Similarly, since you wouldn't lie down in a face-to-face meeting, you should not be reclining in bed or on your couch over teleconferencing either.

Here is a list of "don'ts: for online meetings:

- **Don't multitask:** As tempting as it may be to attend your meeting or online class while using your computer for other purposes, do not do this. First, it is impossible to give your full attention to two tasks simultaneously. By attempting to split your focus between two things, you will not absorb the content of the meeting or class. In addition, you wouldn't be doing work for other areas of your life during a class or meeting if it were in person, so you shouldn't do it on a video call either.

- **Don't log in and leave:** One problem with online meetings and calls is that some participants choose to log into meetings or classes with their camera off and then leave their computer unattended. There are a few things wrong with this scenario. First, if you choose to do this, you will miss the content of the meeting you are attending. Second, your professor can generally tell who is on the call based on participation in discussions, polls, and other opportunities to engage in class. Missing content and lack of participation are two ways in which abandoning your computer during a call can hurt your grades while you are in school, and your relationships with other group members when you begin your career.

JOB APPLICATIONS

Typically, job applications require quite a bit of written exchange, at least initially. In this section, we will introduce you to the most common types of written communication between job seekers and hiring managers: cover letters, resumes, and thank-you notes.

Cover Letters

Cover letters are not always required when applying for jobs, but including a letter with your application will enable you to highlight your strengths and, hopefully, encourage employers to move you to the next stage in the hiring process.

Keep cover letters brief. Feature the reasons why the hiring manager should consider your application. As briefly and specifically as possible, state why you are writing in your opening sentence. Your cover letter should have two other sections that can be separated into paragraphs. The next section should explain why you want the job for which you are applying and should be something other than, "I need a job because my school loans will be due soon." This section should be tailored to the job itself and could include something personal about yourself.

Another section should highlight why you are competent for the posted position. When considering this section, look at the qualifications and/or responsibilities listed in the job posting and emphasize how you can contribute. While you may not have every attribute listed in the job description, your cover letter is a good place to emphasize the required qualifications that you do have. Finally, and in a separate paragraph, thank the recipient of the letter for their time and state what you hope will happen next before your closing and signature.

As with all types of writing, proofread and proofread again before sending out your letter. An effective cover letter is a good demonstration of strong communication skills and will likely help you to stand out in the application process.

Cover Letter Example

A case manager position working with adolescents has become available on a job posting website with the following qualification requirements:

Qualifications:

- Education: MSW or BSW with at least two years of relevant experience, i.e. youth/family interventions, case management, program management. Recent MSW grads encouraged to apply; SIFI certified a plus
- Written and oral proficiency in Spanish required
- Experience working with children and families and with case management and crisis intervention strongly preferred
- Flexible evenings and occasional weekends required in order to meet needs of clients
- Strong interpersonal skills and ability to communicate verbally and in writing to individuals and groups
- Strong presentation and group facilitation skills
- Experience working with volunteer management
- Commitment to helping children, parents and whole families achieve success in life
- Experience with, and knowledge of, NYC not-for-profit agencies and schools a plus
- Demonstrated ability to work in culturally diverse communities
- Ability to multi-task and think systemically
- Proficient with MS Office (particularly with Word, Excel, PowerPoint and Outlook); Knowledge of Zoom platform as well
- Proficient with database entry, data collecting and reporting
- Ability to comply with applicable child safety requirements
- Ability to promote an inclusive, welcoming, and respectful mentoring environment that embraces diversity and inclusion
- Excellent organizational skills, ability to manage caseloads and effectively work with clients

Given the requirements listed above, consider the following sample cover letter:

> Dear Recruiter,
>
> I am writing to apply for the case manager position posted on Idealist.
>
> I believe that I would be a good fit for this position. I am a recent graduate from Berkshire University with an MSW, and I am bilingual in English and Spanish. As you will see in my resume, my first-year field placement involved working with youth and planning after-school activities. The youth in our program came from racially and ethnically diverse neighborhoods and participation in the program helped them do better in school.
>
> In my second-year field placement, I worked in a busy domestic violence shelter where I ran Spanish language groups with mothers and helped connect them to community-based services. In that role, I developed strong organizational skills and regularly made notes in the agency's electronic record-keeping system.
>
> For two summers, I also worked at a summer camp with middle school-aged children. Based on these experiences, I am certain that I would like to pursue work with adolescents in my professional experiences.
>
> I believe I am a good candidate to work at XYZ Agency. Thank you for your time and consideration. I look forward to hearing from you to learn more about the case manager position.
>
> Sincerely,
> New Graduate

Can you identify the following aspects of the cover letter above?

- An explanation of why you are writing.
- A description of what interests you about the job or why you are applying.
- Information that demonstrates why you are competent for the position, accentuating skills that were identified as essential in the job description.
- Thanks to the recipient and a statement of what you hope will happen next.

Writing Exercise 3.2

Working with a partner (another student, a field director, or a person in your school's career center) or on your own, find a job you might be interested in applying for, now or in the future, and write a cover letter applying for the job:

- After drafting your letter, use the following checklist to see that you have:
  1 included the purpose for writing in the first sentence;
  2 included a paragraph on why you are applying for the job;
  3 included a paragraph explaining why you are qualified for the position; and
  4 included a concluding paragraph thanking the recipient and stating what you think should happen next.
- Proofread your letter aloud: are you communicating your ideas in the best way possible? Edit the text to make sure your message is clear.
- Proofread your letter aloud AGAIN. This time, check for standard punctuation, grammar, tense, and capitalization.
- Do one of the following:
  1 If you are working with a partner, ask for feedback. Does your partner think the letter could be sent out as written or do they have ideas for improving it?
  2 If you are working on your own, consider the following question: if you were the hiring manager and received this letter from someone you didn't know, would you invite that person to continue in the hiring process? Use your honest assessment to make edits to this letter.

Resumes

Resumes contain a brief synopsis of your educational and employment background, and may contain a statement about your professional goals. It is important to present a polished resume, as this is often the first thing that hiring managers see about you.

At the end of this chapter, we share several resources to help you write that perfect resume; but be aware that well-written resumes should have the following characteristics:

- **They should be short:** Hiring managers want to look at a resume briefly and determine whether the applicant could be a good fit for the job. Use the space wisely to demonstrate your accomplishments.

- **They should be well edited:** Grammatical errors, hard-to-read fonts, and inconsistent spacing send a negative message. Conversely, brief, consistently formatted resumes convey professionalism.
- **They should contain relevant, up-to-date information:** Make sure your contact information is current and your email address appears professional. Include job or volunteer experiences that demonstrate your involvement in the community or area in which you want to work.

An example of a well-written resume for a new graduate can be found in Appendix C.

Thank-You Emails

Whether it is a phone interview, a meeting over Zoom, or an in-person interview, it is good form to send a thank-you note to each person you meet during the recruitment process. These emails can be brief, but should include the following:

- the person's name—if you are not sure how to address them, use formal salutations like "Ms.," "Mr." or "Dr.";
- a thank-you for their time;
- a brief mention of something you discussed or learned about in your meeting; and
- a polite closing with an expectation that you will meet again.

Below is an example of a thank-you email based upon the case manager position described previously.

> Dear Mr. Smith,
>
> Thank you for meeting with me last Tuesday to discuss the case manager position.
> After meeting with you, I am certain that I would be a good fit for this job. I am particularly drawn to your description of the work itself, and I find the emphasis on group work in line with my own professional goals.

Thank you again for your time and consideration. I look forward to meeting you in person shortly.

Sincerely,
New Graduate

In this example, note each of the following elements:

- addressing the recipient by name;
- thanking the recipient for their time;
- a reference to something you discussed or learned from your meeting; and
- a closing that sets the expectations for a future meeting.

Writing Exercise 3.3

Consider the job you applied for in Exercise 3.2. Imagine you had an initial Zoom interview with this potential employer and write a thank-you note for the interview.

- After drafting your note, use the following checklist to see that you have:
  1. included the individual's name;
  2. thanked them for the time they spent with you;
  3. mentioned something that you discussed with them; and
  4. included a closing that assumes you will meet again.
- Proofread your letter aloud. Are you communicating the ideas you want to communicate in the best way possible? Edit the text to make sure your message is clear.
- Proofread your letter aloud AGAIN. This time, check for standard punctuation, grammar, tense, and capitalization.
- Do one of the following:
  1. If you are working with a partner, ask for feedback. Does your partner think the letter could be sent out as written or do they have ideas for improving it?
  2. If you are working on your own, consider the following question: if you were the hiring manager and received this letter from someone you didn't know, would you invite that person to continue in the hiring process? Use your honest assessment to make edits to this letter.

MISCELLANEOUS LETTERS

Once in the field, you may also need to write actual letters that will be sent using "snail mail." In other instances, it may be necessary to send a formal letter as an attachment to an email. As always, you should begin this type of writing by explaining who you are and why you are writing. You may provide a lot more information, but you should always include what you would like to happen as a result of your correspondence. For example, you may need to advocate for clients you serve by writing to a legislator. In this case, you may start your letter by stating:

> *I am a social worker at the homeless shelter in your district, and I am writing to you because we are noticing an increasing number of families requesting housing each month. This letter is to alert you to the growing homeless population in your district and the need for services for these families.*

A concluding paragraph could state:

> *In short, it is my professional opinion that passage of H.B. 1075 is necessary for the well-being of your constituents, and I hope that you intend to support it.*

Notice that the first sentence indicates who you are and the basic reason for writing. The second sentence explains what the remainder of the letter will be about: the needs of homeless families in the legislator's district. Your conclusion indicates what you would like to happen: the legislator's support for a specific bill.

CONCLUSION

In this chapter, we covered communication that often goes beyond the classroom. It is important to emphasize that email, texts, online meetings, and letters are often your first point of contact with individuals who may not know you well, or at all. Therefore, it is important to make a good first impression. As we discussed earlier in this chapter, and as you will see repeatedly throughout this book, you should always present yourself professionally. This means being fully aware of how you are perceived in a Zoom meeting or in writing. One relatively quick and easy way to do this is to carefully proofread all written communications that you send.

Quick Tips: Writing Checklist

- Consider your audience.
- Explain who you are and why you're writing.
- Clearly communicate what you would like to be the result of your letter or email.
- Be careful about how you are communicating.
- Consider how your message will be perceived.
- Be concise and informative.
- Proofread your messages.

FURTHER INFORMATION

Emails to Professors

- Northern Illinois University's Center for Innovative Teaching and Learning shares tips for effective communication with your professors via email. This guide, called *Emailing Your Professor,* clarifies when an email to your professor would be most effective and when a face-to-face or Zoom conversation would be more appropriate:
  https://www.niu.edu/citl/resources/guides/students/emailing-your-professor.shtml

- If you do send an email to your professor, you want it to be read. *Emailing your College Professor: Do's and Don'ts*, from U.S. News.com, emphasizes the importance of only sending emails to your instructors from your college or university account. It also demonstrates why a clear and concise email subject line increases the chances that your professors will see and then read emails you send to them:
  https://www.usnews.com/education/articles/emailing-your-college-professor-dos-and-donts

Workplace Emails

- This article from Indeed, entitled *28 Best Practices for Email Etiquette in the Workplace*, covers the top tips for workplace email etiquette, including formatting, tone, and word choice:
https://www.indeed.com/career-advice/career-development/email-etiquette
- TopResume.com offers advice for writing concise, professional emails that your recipient will want to read and respond to in its article *Email Etiquette: 11 Email Communication Best Practices*:
https://www.topresume.com/career-advice/best-practices-email-etiquette-work
- *The Dos and Don'ts of Business Email Etiquette*, an article on Grammarly.com, highlights the importance of being sensitive to culture in your business email communications:
https://www.grammarly.com/blog/business-email-etiquette/

Zoom Meeting Etiquette

- *Zoom Etiquette for Students – 12 Easy-to-Follow Rules* is a comprehensive guide from Sembly AI on how students can effectively use Zoom and other video platforms to enhance online classroom experiences. While this article pitches their own product, the tips they provide are helpful to everyone, regardless of whether you purchase their tool:
https://www.sembly.ai/blog/zoom-etiquette-for-students-12-easy-to-follow-rules/
- The article *8 Zoom Etiquette Rules Everyone Should Follow*, from Entrepreneur.com, suggests that the success of your online meetings can be boosted by a little advance preparation:
https://www.entrepreneur.com/science-technology/8-zoom-etiquette-rules-everyone-should-follow/383772
- The University of the Potomac's online article entitled *Online Etiquette: 14 Netiquette Rules Online Students Should Know* shares best practices for students in online classes:
https://potomac.edu/netiquette-rules-online-students/

Business Letters

- *How to Write a Business Letter*, by the editorial team at Indeed, not only explains the reasons you would want to send a business letter, but also provides you with a template and example to guide you in writing your own business letter: https://ie.indeed.com/career-advice/career-development/how-to-write-business-letter

- Purdue Online Writing Lab has created an in-depth instructional resource on proper business letter format. Its article entitled *Writing the Basic Business Letter* covers appropriate use of salutations, font, and punctuation for professional letter writing: https://owl.purdue.edu/owl/subject_specific_writing/professional_technical_writing/basic_business_letters/index.html

- In addition to explaining the proper format for a business letter, Microsoft's article *How to Write (and Format) a Successful Business Letter* addresses the importance of keeping business letters concise and direct: https://www.microsoft.com/en-us/microsoft-365-life-hacks/writing/writing-a-business-letter

Professional Text Messages

- The blog post *10 Professional Texting Etiquette Rules*, from the HuffPost Contributor platform, offers tips to ensure that you present yourself in the most professional manner when sending text messages to clients, supervisors, and colleagues. https://www.huffpost.com/entry/10-professional-texting-e_b_12154416

- *Rules of Office Texting Etiquette*, a blog post from the company Simple Texting, emphasizes that text messaging can make workplace communication more efficient, provided that texts remain professional in tone and content: https://simpletexting.com/rules-of-office-texting-etiquette/#:~:text=That%20being%20said%2C%20there%20are%20some%20foundational%20text, without%20a%20response%20unless%20otherwise%20directed.%20More%20items

Cover Letters

- Harvard Business Review's article entitled *How to Write a Cover Letter* explains how to grab the attention of a hiring manager with a cover letter that expresses your enthusiasm for the position you are applying for, while also describing how you would add value to the organization if you were hired: https://hbr.org/2014/02/how-to-write-a-cover-letter
- *How To Write a Cover Letter (With Steps, Examples and Tips)*, from Indeed, teaches you how to write a cover letter in six clear steps. If you are concerned about how best to format your letter, this article is a great place to start. https://www.indeed.com/career-advice/resumes-cover-letters/how-to-write-a-cover-letter
- Some recruitment platforms may not specify that you need to include a cover letter. However, even in those instances, a well-written cover letter sent by email to the hiring manager can be the difference between getting an interview and being overlooked as a candidate. Glassdoor's blog post *Emailing a Cover Letter: How To Guide with Example* walks you through the most effective way to email your cover letter to a prospective employer: https://www.glassdoor.com/blog/guide/emailing-a-cover-letter/

Resumes

- If you have never written a resume before, the ZipRecruiter blog post *How to Write Your First Resume* can help to demystify resume writing. The ZipRecruiter Team shows you how to get started creating your first resume even when you have limited work experience: https://www.ziprecruiter.com/blog/how-to-write-your-first-resume/
- Monster offers a comprehensive guide to writing your resume in its aptly titled article, *How to Write a Resume*. It links you to multiple resources on resume strategy, the components of a great resume and the gaffes to avoid when writing your resume. https://www.monster.com/career-advice/article/how-to-write-a-resume

Thank-You Letters

- The Indeed editorial team suggest tips for writing a thank-you letter to a professor or former employer who has written a letter of recommendation on your behalf in *Writing a Thank You-Email For a Letter of Recommendation.* The article includes a number of sample thank-you letters to inspire you in your own letter writing:
  https://ca.indeed.com/career-advice/resumes-cover-letters/thank-you-email-for-letter-of-recommendation

- The Muse knows that sometimes you will want to go the extra mile in a thank-you note to show your interviewer that you were listening carefully and are a good fit for the team you interviewed to join. *A Template for the Perfect Thank-You Email After an Interview (Plus Samples!)* offers examples of thank-you letters to help you continue to make a good impression on the hiring manager:
  https://www.themuse.com/advice/how-to-write-an-interview-thankyou-note-an-email-template

USING TECHNOLOGY TO MAKE WRITING EASIER

INTRODUCTION

Thirty years ago, the use of technology to help with writing generally involved using electric typewriters or word processors on home computers to make writing more legible. Today, there are myriad tools available to help you organize your writing and references, provide access to documents, and assist with common issues like spelling and grammar. In this chapter, we will identify resources that you may find helpful with all these things. It is likely that you are aware of many of these tools; however, some may be new to you. Additionally, resources that you currently use may have useful functions that you are unaware of. In Chapter 4 of this book, detailed descriptions of writing assisting software are provided, together with the web addresses for accessing them.

In this chapter, we will begin by discussing information literacy and library resources. From there, we will explain how to make the most of your word processing software—whether it be Microsoft Word, Google Docs, or something else. Then, we will move on to solutions for creating accurate bibliographies; and finally, we will give you hints for storing and retrieving your documents.

INFORMATION LITERACY AND YOUR LIBRARY

In university settings and among professionals, there is an increasing need to be able to find, understand, and use information effectively and efficiently. Despite this, most graduate students do not use librarians or library resources regularly, unless they are located online (Association for College & Research Libraries, 2015; Harrington, 2009).

DOI: 10.4324/9781003168713-5

In your quest to become a better writer, you will almost certainly need to gather and synthesize information. Making use of your library's resources is a great place to begin improving your skills. While each school's library is different, many have similar features that we will share with you here. As we go through this section, we encourage you to use your school's website to follow along, to see what is available to you. Your brick-and-mortar library will also have additional assets such as hard copies of books and copies of older journal articles.

Librarians

Your school's librarians are specialists in accessing and using information. These are resources that are often overlooked by students who are used to searching for information online or do not often go to a brick-and-mortar library. If you have questions related to research, accessing resources, or finding books or articles, reach out to a school librarian in one of three ways:

- **Go to the library:** If you go to any service desk and ask to speak to a librarian, you will be pointed in the right direction.
- **Visit your library's website:** From the home page, most schools have a link that will connect you to a live chat with a librarian.
- **On your library's website, search for a librarian who is a liaison for your course of study:** You can often find the topics and/or programs in which librarians specialize in the section where you find research guides. Alternatively, some libraries provide a list of librarians and their specialties. Subject-matter expert librarians and program liaisons are particularly helpful if you have a specialized question; however, our experience is that most librarians can answer most questions. If they are unable to assist you, they will direct you to subject-matter specialists.

Research Guides

Most university libraries produce research guides that are available to students on the first page of the library's website. A research guide is a curated collection of texts, websites, journals, and other sources of information that research librarians and faculty think would be helpful to a course of study, such as social work, or to all students more generally. When you access your library's research guide page, orient yourself by exploring all research guides that may be relevant to you. For example, master's of social work students in our program are encouraged to explore the following research guides:

- General (contains links to information about cultural information and open educational resources);
- Government Information (contains links to information about U.S. immigration and the federal government);
- News and Newspapers (contains links to the university's subscription to major newspapers);
- Research and Writing (contains links to citation tools and career research);
- Library Services & Events (contains information for alumni library resources and a guide for graduate students); and
- Statistics (contains links to statistical data for the state, county, and city).

Additionally, the Social Work research guide provides links to books, ebooks, open-access textbooks, videos, evidence-based resources, and databases that are particularly relevant to social work students. In short, research guides are great starting points for narrowing down the breadth of library resources available to you.

Books

You can look for books on your library's website, which will allow you use filters to narrow your search. While print books may be available in the physical library, ebooks can be accessed online.

Journal Articles

When you need to read or utilize journal articles for assignments, your professor will most likely require you to use peer-reviewed articles. Peer review is a rigorous process by which manuscripts are critiqued by experts in the field, usually through a blind process where neither the manuscript authors nor the reviewers know who the others are. As a result, manuscript reviewers have the freedom to offer constructive criticism on all aspects of an article prior to publication, and journal editors can require extensive editing or even reject the publication of articles as a result of the peer-review process. Peer-reviewed articles, which are described in detail in Chapter 1, are considered the gold standard of academic rigor and are viewed as more scholarly than textbooks.

Again, your library's website and research guides are a good starting point for finding relevant peer-reviewed journal articles through searches of specific journals or databases. Database search pages allow you to use specific search criteria to narrow the results. You will want to do so as much as possible, as search criteria that are too broad will result in thousands or millions of articles that you will need to wade through. A successful search for articles may take some time and is often an iterative process where you continue narrowing the results until you have a reasonable number of articles to review. Suggestions for conducting a successful search include the following:

- **Limit your search to peer-reviewed articles:** Many databases provide access to different types of articles, so be sure to indicate in your search criteria (usually with a check box) that you only want to view peer-reviewed articles.
- **Limit the publication date of articles:** Usually, you will want the most current research on a particular topic. You can limit your results to articles published in the last five or 10 years; if this is the case, put your starting year at the earliest date desired and leave the end date blank. Check with your professor to determine what their requirements are.
- **Play around with search terms:** Most database searches enable you to use multiple words or phrases to conduct your search using Boolean operators. This enables robust searching by allowing you to use quotation marks to search for exact phrases, and terms such as AND, OR, and NOT to help narrow your search.
- **Limit your search to full texts and PDFs:** PDFs allow you to view an entire article exactly as it looks in print. This can be helpful when you are citing a direct quotation and need page numbers. You may want to save downloaded PDFs for possible use in future assignments. Software described in Chapter 5 can assist with creating your own libraries of your resources.

Interlibrary Loans

Your school library likely has access to many journals, books, and periodicals; but no academic library has everything. Most academic libraries can, however, loan you books, articles, book chapters, and more from other sources. From your library home page, search for "interlibrary loans." Once you have found the designated page, easy-to-follow instructions should enable you to request the materials you want, most of which can be delivered electronically. Don't wait until the last minute because this may take several days.

WORD PROCESSING SOFTWARE AND DOCUMENT STORAGE

Word processing software is used by every student to take notes, write papers, and more. It is a necessity for accomplishing tasks for school. In this section, we will address how to choose the right software package for your needs and avail yourself of its most useful features.

Microsoft Word

Most schools give students access to key Microsoft products, including Word and Excel, for free or at greatly reduced prices. A search from your school's homepage for "student software" and/or "IT services" will likely point you in the right direction.

Microsoft Word can be customized to do almost anything imaginable and has features that most free programs do not have. We will highlight a few helpful options here, but this list is not exhaustive. If you want to do something and are unsure if you can do it in Word, a quick Google search should help you out.

Features that students often find useful can be found in the *Tools* option in the toolbar. Here you can check your word count and access a thesaurus, among other tasks. The *Spell Check* function points out spelling errors as you go with a red squiggle, while grammar errors are double-underlined in blue. *Track Changes* allows you to see edits in your document as you work. With the *New Comment* function you can jot down ideas as you work.

One lesser-used feature in Microsoft Word is the dictation function. When you enable *Dictate*, you can simply speak into your computer and the text will appear on your screen. You may have to go back and edit it, but with Dictate you can quickly get your ideas down if that is your preferred way of preparing for assignments. This option can be found on the Home tab.

Another feature that may be useful is the Read Aloud option, found in the Review tab. In Chapter 1, we suggested that you read your assignments aloud prior to submitting them to ensure that you have written what you intended. The Read Aloud feature enables you to do just that with precision.

There are times when your computer may crash (!) or you may forget to save a document. When this happens, all is not lost! If you store your documents in OneDrive, be sure to enable "Turn on AutoSave by Default" in Word Preferences. If you do not use One-Drive, you can set up a preference so documents are saved periodically through the AutoRecover function on your computer. For more details on how to utilize these options, visit docs.microsoft.com or do a Google search.

As you write your papers, you can insert citations using the Insert Citation function under the References tab. If you click the Citations function, you can view all items cited within your document. Finally, you can create your reference page at the end of your assignment by selecting Bibliography.

Google Docs

Today, many students use Google Docs to create documents and collaborate with other students—and this is a great idea! One advantage to using Google Docs is that multiple people can access the same document simultaneously to add content or make edits; and all edits you make are automatically saved, so your document will never be accidentally deleted.

Documents can also be downloaded into a variety of formats, including those compatible with creating webpages (.html), Microsoft Word (.docx), or as a PDF (.pdf).

Google Docs has many similar features to those found in Microsoft Word. For example, instead of Track Changes, Google Docs has a Suggesting mode. Since changes to documents are automatically saved, one helpful feature in Google Docs is the ability to view and revert to previous versions of a document. This option can be found in the File menu.

Another nice feature for students is the ability to add citations in APA 7th Edition style. Access to this option can be found in the Tools menu. While you can create both in-text citations and bibliographies with the Citations feature, be aware that the citations you create are stored in the document you are using and are not readily transferable to other documents.

Dropbox

While Dropbox is not word processing software, it allows you to store all types of files—including spreadsheets, photos, and data—online. These files can then be accessed from anywhere you have an internet connection.

With Dropbox, you can set up files and documents just as you would on your computer. This allows you to organize your documents in whatever way works best for you (e.g., by semester or by class); and you can share files and documents however you would like. For instance, you can email classmates a link to a file with all your presentation materials, but not allow them to edit the documents. They can then download the materials and edit them before emailing their changes to you. You can also share a folder with classmates, asking everyone to contribute various documents to that folder. This helps you stay organized and keeps everything that goes together in the same place.

Once you have set up a Dropbox account, you can download the application to your computer so you can view files stored in Dropbox in the same way as you view all other files. They will sync automatically to your online Dropbox account when you save files, provided you have an internet connection. If you are offline, your files will sync with your Dropbox account when you regain an internet connection. Another advantage to using Dropbox is the ability to view and restore previous versions of a document. This can be especially helpful if you are using Microsoft Word and your computer crashes, or if you make substantial changes to any document and want to undo those changes. Finally, deleted documents can easily be restored by accessing your Dropbox account online.

Currently, Dropbox allows you to store 2 gigabytes of data at no cost. More information can be found at www.dropbox.com.

Writing Exercise 4.1

Working with a partner or on your own, locate and explore research guides for social work and related disciplines on your library's website. Search for peer-reviewed journal articles related to an upcoming assignment.

If you are able, visit your institution's library with your partner and meet with a librarian who specializes in social sciences. While there, locate texts relevant to social work or which your professors may have put on reserve. If you are working on your own, you can complete the first three parts of this exercise.

- Make notes on the information that you gather from your sources utilizing your preferred word processing software.
- Note your sources within your word processing software so you can credit them appropriately.
- Use the Read Aloud function in your word processing software to proofread your notes.
- Create a shared Google Drive or Dropbox account with your partner.
- Share your notes with each other via your chosen document storage account. Experiment with giving each other read-only and editor-level access within your documents
- Give feedback to each other using the Comment tool for your word processing software.
- Reflect with each other on the ease or difficulty of each step of this writing exercise, and seek guidance from a librarian or instructor as needed.

CONCLUSION

This chapter explained how you can use your computer and internet connection to work for you to become a more adept researcher and writer. As you become more immersed in your classes, fieldwork, and assignments, the library resources and other available resources we discussed should be helpful to you.

Quick Tips: Libraries and Documents

- Visit and explore your school library's website.
- Locate and explore research guides for social work and related disciplines on the website.

- Learn how to search for hard copies and ebooks.
- Explore and experiment with searching for journals and peer-reviewed journal articles.
- Search for and learn how to apply for an interlibrary loan.
- Look into helpful features on your preferred word processing software. Choose whether you want to store your school documents on Google Drive, Dropbox, locally on your own computer, or on some other cloud-based service.

FURTHER INFORMATION

Information Literacy and Your Library

- Oxford Royale Academy's article entitled *8 Ways to Get the Most Out of Your University Library* suggests that early on in your academic journey, you should tour your institution's library, familiarize yourself with the Dewey Decimal System, and use the library's group study spaces to increase your effectiveness as a student:
  https://www.oxford-royale.com/articles/university-library/
- Northwestern University Libraries has created a resource, called *Start Your Research*, to guide you through the research process. This includes tips to help you develop your research question, locate sources you will use to answer the research question, and identify methods for analyzing and recording your sources:
  https://libguides.northwestern.edu/start-research/step-by-step
- Peer-reviewed journal articles are the highest standard in scholarly literature. Sometimes it is hard to distinguish peer-reviewed article from other types of literature. *FAQ: How Can I Determine if a Journal is Peer Reviewed?*, from the Shapiro Library at Southern New Hampshire University, can help you determine if an article is peer reviewed:
  https://libanswers.snhu.edu/faq/86723
- Likewise, Angelo State University provides guidance to help you confirm that a journal article is peer reviewed before you include it in your assignment in an article titled *Library Guides: How to Recognize Peer-Reviewed (Refereed) Journals*:
  https://www.angelo.edu/library/handouts/peTrrev.php

- *How to Use Technology to Write Better Papers*, from IT Phobia, suggests tips for using technology to help you brainstorm, research, and draft your papers. The article also offers helpful hints to avoid plagiarism:
  https://itphobia.com/?s=how+to+use+technology
- Lastly, Montclair State University has curated several video tutorials to help you sharpen your database research skills—including how to use Boolean operators—on its page entitled *Tutorials and How-To Videos*.
  https://montclair.libguides.com/c.php?g=297296&p=1981314

THE BASICS OF APA
WRITING STYLE

INTRODUCTION

Social work research, clinical papers, and reports require the use of references and citations that inform the reader of the sources of the information presented. At the time of writing, the American Psychological Association's (APA) *Publication Manual, Seventh Edition* is used as a guide to references and citations. The manual can be purchased in a variety of formats. Additionally, online resources are listed, most of which are free and easily accessible.

This chapter provides a roadmap for using many of the APA 7th Edition elements of scholarly style. It is not meant to be a substitution for the full manual, but rather a quick-use guide that may be sufficient for new social work students and those with more experience who would like an expeditious review.

USING CITATIONS TO CREDIT PUBLISHED SOURCES

Imagine spending hours writing an article only for someone to take exact quotes from your work and sign their name to it. Alternatively, they might not take your exact words, but still present the ideas formulated in your article as their own. That doesn't seem fair—and it isn't. There is a term for taking someone else's work without giving them credit: "plagiarism." To give credit where it is due, we use citations and references. We will begin this chapter with a discussion of citations.

The format for citations used in social work writing follows the APA 7th Edition style. Assignments in social work often ask students

DOI: 10.4324/9781003168713-6

to refer both to class readings in textbooks and to what are sometimes referred to as "outside readings." These outside readings will likely be published articles from academic journals or media sources. When writing about ideas expressed in these sources, we need to cite the author(s) in the text (body) of the paper. In this section, we will cover the most common types of citations found in social work assignments. For a complete list of citation styles used in writing academic papers, please consult the *Manual* (APA, 2020) or refer to the websites listed at the end of this chapter.

Citation Rules

When using direct quotations or paraphrasing from published works (e.g., articles; books; government reports; media sources; legal documents, including laws and legal commentary; religious documents; visual sources such as videos or PowerPoints; and all other sources of information), you will need to cite the authors, if available, or the title of the sources if the authors' names are unavailable. In other words, you will need to cite every source which you quote. Personal conversations that add to the information you are writing about must also be cited.

In addition to direct quotes, paraphrased or summarized writing often requires a citation. Sometimes students describe an author's central thesis in their own words instead of using the exact words in a published work. This is known as "paraphrasing," and a citation at either the beginning or the end of the paraphrased idea is needed to give credit when due. Usually, you will need to include a citation once in each paragraph where you discuss the author's central idea, unless you interject another author's idea in between repeated references to a specific work.

The examples in Table 5.1 illustrate the most common citation types you will need to insert in the body of your papers.

When the author of a report or an online post is unknown, use the title of the organization sponsoring the report or webpage—for example: (National Organization of Social Workers, [NASW] 2020). After the first long citation, you may use the abbreviation for the organization: (NASW, 2020). If you take a direct quote from a webpage or document with no page numbers, use the term "para," indicating the paragraph number: (NASW, 2020, para. 2).

Table 5.1 Common Citation Types

Author(s)	Citation
One author (ideas, paraphrased)	(Jones, 2020)
One author (direct quote)	(Jones, 2020, p.32)
Two authors	(Jones & Smith, 2020)
Three or more authors	(Jones et al., 2020)
Organization, no author	(National Organization of Social Workers, [NASW], 2020)
If more than one page on a direct quote or paraphrase, use pp.	(Jones, 2020, pp. 24–26)
When citing more than one author, list alphabetically	(Jones, 2020; Smith, 2022)

You may ask, "How many times do I need to cite an author when I use their work throughout my paper?" It is necessary to include a citation after each direct quotation. When paraphrasing, you can first cite the author where it makes most sense to do so. You can then repeat the citation in the next paragraph where you include the author's ideas. In other words, when paraphrasing, you need only cite once in any paragraph. The exception to this rule is if the paraphrasing is interrupted by a quote from or paraphrasing of another author. Over-citation can result in a choppy writing style; but while it may not be the best way of communicating your ideas, it is still better than not citing and risking plagiarism. It is usually a good idea to reread your assignments and, if possible, ask another person with writing experience to read your work before submission.

Here is a brief example of citations used in a paragraph. An additional example of an academic paper is provided in Appendix A of this book.

Many consider schizophrenia to be the epitome of a severe mental illness (SMI) (Hofmann & Tompson, 2002). Characterized by hallucinations, delusions, and other psychotic symptoms (American Psychiatric Association, 2000), schizophrenia frequently has a deleterious influence on various aspects of idiographic functioning (Hofmann & Tompson, 2002).

Schizophrenia is associated with lack of employment (Rosenheck et al., 2006), increased risk for homelessness (Folsom & Jeste, 2002), as well as marital discord (Hooley et al., 1987). Symptoms of schizophrenia are linked to impairment in academic performance, daily living activities, parenting, and social relationships (Mueser & McGurk, 2004). In the United States, approximately 5 out of 1000 people are diagnosed with schizophrenia (Wu et al., 2006). After neuroleptics began to show an ability to decrease positive symptoms, treatment of schizophrenia switched from psychodynamic therapy to biologically based interventions (Pratt & Mueser, 2002). Currently, the United States views neuroleptic (antipsychotic) treatment as the fundamental aspect of intervention for schizophrenia (Turkington et al., 2006).

Adapted from: Gregory, V.L. Jr. (2010) Cognitive-Behavioral Therapy for schizophrenia: Applications to social work practice. *Social Work in Mental Health, 8*(2), 140-159, DOI: 10.1080/15332980902791086

CREATING THE REFERENCES PAGE

The section of your assigned paper where you list the sources of your paper's information is titled "References." Students sometimes mistakenly use terms such as "Bibliography," "Works cited," or "REFERENCES." APA 7th Edition style requires that the title "References" be written in bold and placed in the center of the page. The references should be in the same font and size as the other sections of your written text, and formatted in what is known as a "hanging style," where the first line is flush with the left margin with the remaining lines indented five spaces. The entire list should be double spaced, and entries should be listed alphabetically by the last name of the first author.

Most references are typically published articles or books; but they can also be personal interviews, media reports and presentations, videos, photographs, and any other sources of information cited in your paper. The important point to keep in mind is that the references on your list must be cited in your paper and vice versa; all in-text citations must be included in the reference list. Sources you may have used but did not cite should not be included in the reference list.

The format for listing references is illustrated in the box below and should be followed as closely as possible. There will be times when you do not have all the information called for by APA 7th Edition style. If this occurs, simply leave out the missing information; or if a publication date is unavailable, add "(n.d.)" in parentheses after the author's name (e.g., "Jones (n.d.)"). If you are writing for publication, you might want to consult the *Publication Manual*. For class assignments and most term papers, this is likely to be unnecessary; simply leave out any information you do not have.

References are listed in alphabetical order by the first letter of the first author's last name. When you have more than one article or book by the same author, references are arranged by the publication date, with the newest first. The symbol "&" is used instead of the word "and" before the last author listed in any one reference. Looking at the examples in the box below, notice that the date follows the authors and is enclosed in parentheses. In the title of the article, only the first letter of the first word in the title is written in upper case. If there is a colon in the title, the first letter of the first word after the colon is written in upper case. The remaining words in the title are written in lower case unless proper nouns are included in the title. The name of the journal or book is italicized, followed by the volume number (e.g., "*30*"), which is also italicized. If there is an issue number, it follows the volume number, it is enclosed in parentheses but is not italicized; similarly, page numbers, which follow the volume/issue number, are not italicized. Finally, the DOI or URL is written just as it appears in the article information. These digital representations assist the reader in locating online editions of the article. It is best to use your computer to copy DOIs and URLs instead of trying to write them out on your own.

For some students, the description above may appear complicated, with details that are difficult to remember. Examples of references may be easier to refer to when writing your reference list.

Here is an example of a short reference page.

References

Bentall, R.P., Corcoran, R., Howard, R., Blackwood, N., & Kinderman, P. (2001). Persecutory delusions: A review and theoretical integration.

Clinical Psychology Review, 21(8), 1143–1192. doi:10.1016/S0272–7358(01)00106-4

Bentall, R.P., Kinderman, P., & Kaney, S. (1994). The self, attributional processes and abnormal beliefs: Towards a model of persecutory delusions. *Behaviour Research and Therapy, 22*(3), 331–341. doi:10.1016/0005–7967(94)90131-7

Berger, C.S. (2002). Social work case-management in medical settings. In A.R. Roberts, & G.J. Greene (Eds.), *Social worker's desk reference* (pp. 497–501). Oxford University Press.

Bieling, P.J., McCabe, R.E., & Antony, M.M. (2006). *Cognitive-behavioral therapy in groups*. Guilford Press.

Birchwood, M. & Chadwick, P., (1997). The omnipotence of voices: Testing the validity of a cognitive model. *Psychological Medicine, 27,* 1345–1353. doi:10.1017/S0033291797005552

Birchwood, M. & Jackson, C., (2001). *Schizophrenia*. Taylor & Francis.

*Adapted from: Gregory, V.L. Jr. (2010) Cognitive-Behavioral Therapy for schizophrenia: Applications to social work practice. *Social Work in Mental Health, 8*(2), 140–159, DOI: 10.1080/15332980902791086

Using Software Can Help

There are a variety of programs that can create a reference page if you provide the sources (e.g., journals, books, reports) and type them into the program's portal. When using any program, be sure to select APA 7th Edition reference style, as it may be programmed for a variety of writing styles. Here are a few programs that you may be interested in using. The URLs for these software programs are listed at the end of this chapter.

- **Zotero:** Zotero stores downloaded citation information and documents, and arranges a reference list for you as you select them for your assignment. Information on using Zotero can be found on the organization's website. The basic program is free and is embedded in the later versions of Microsoft Word. You will find it on the top banner of the program. If you use Google Docs or older versions of Word, you will need to download it.

When using the reference tool, be sure to select APA 7th Edition as your preferred reference style. Zotero creates a library arranged and labeled by the subjects you choose for its headings. Your library then becomes available to you for future assignments. Zotero can also search for websites.

- **EndNote:** EndNote creates a library for your references, assists in searching for new references, inserts citations and creates a reference list. There is a fee, although many schools offer EndNote to students without charge. Ask your librarian if your school subscribes to the software program and provides instruction on its use.

- **Mendeley Cite:** This software program is offered as a free add-in for Word. It creates citations and references as you write and stores them for future use. You can create an account or use the add-in for Word function on its website. The web address for Mendeley Cite includes instructions on how to add it into Word or create a separate account.

It is a good idea to select a program that your university, its library, and your computer management department are familiar with and can support. You may want to check on your computer management department's website to see if EndNote and Mendeley Cite are listed. As noted above, Zotero can be used by anyone writing in Word and Google Docs. EndNote offers a free 30-day trial service, after which there is a fee. Mendeley Cite is also free for Word users with Microsoft software and Windows versions later than 2016. The above information related to accessibility and charges can change at any time, so it is best to check the relevant software website for the most up-to-date information.

GETTING HELP FROM WEBSITES FOR CITATIONS AND REFERENCES

There are also websites that may be helpful—the most popular are listed below. You can do your own search by typing "APA 7th Edition" into your search engine. Because URLs can change along with their content, you may find doing your own search to be your best option. The websites discussed below can be found at the end of this chapter.

APA 7ᵗʰ Edition Style, Student Paper Setup Guide

The *APA 7ᵗʰ Edition Style Student Paper Setup Guide,* published by the APA, offers a full-scale display for setting up papers. The descriptions are easy to follow, and most are enhanced with illustrations. The guide even includes a checklist for you to scroll through to be sure your use of APA 7ᵗʰ Edition style is correct. For your convenience, this is included at the end of this chapter.

APA 7ᵗʰ Edition References on the APA Website

The *APA Reference Guide* helps with grammar and setting up references, and is available on the site listed at the end of this chapter. The *Paper Setup Guide* mentioned above can answer most questions you may have; but if you have a source that needs referencing which is not covered in the *Paper Setup Guide*, this is the resource for you. It addresses just about any type of resource and configuration that you can think of. As you scroll down the page, you will find links to a variety of reference types. There is even a link to a *Common Reference Examples Guide*, which we list for you to download for future use.

Purdue Online Writing Lab

Purdue University's *Online Writing Lab*, also known as the Purdue OWL, is a popular website for students and is constructed to be user friendly. It provides useful resources for all sorts of writing skills, including APA 7ᵗʰ Edition style. There is an extensive list of reference types; and an APA Citation Reference Machine that lets you type in your citation to see how it should appear in APA 7ᵗʰ Edition style. The use of the premium citation machine does come with a fee. Still, there is plenty of free information available, with illustrated examples and even some videos for those who are visual learners.

Grammarly Basic and Grammarly Premium

Grammarly Basic provides guides to grammar and spelling by tagging errors and suggesting corrections. It is easy to use and is an effective way to polish your writing for everyday use. Grammarly Premium offers suggestions for rewriting sentences to achieve enhanced clarity. It also offers a plagiarism checker and can generate citations in multiple formats. You can use both versions of the software together or separately. There is no charge for Grammarly Basic. Once you begin using Grammarly Basic, you may be offered access to Grammarly Premium if your school has an agreement with the software company. Basic is embedded in Google Docs and can be downloaded to Word. The address for accessing it is listed at the end of this chapter.

Example Paper from Antioch University

We provide a link to an example of a paper available through Antioch University in Appendix A of this book; the link is also included at the end of this chapter. This paper is a good "cheat sheet," in that it highlights what you should do to format all aspects of a paper in proper APA 7th Edition style. Check it out! It may be a good fit for your learning style.

SUBJECT HEADINGS

Subject headings at the beginning of a new paragraph guide the reader through your work. They serve as a way of emphasizing important ideas you want to share. Using headings throughout your paper helps organize the basic ideas you are presenting. It makes your paper user friendly and acts as a kind of roadmap for the reader to follow.

Paragraph Headings

The best way to master the use of paragraph headings is to use the examples shown in Table 5.2. You might want to place a bookmark on this page to refer to it when you get to the final draft of your paper.

Tips on Heading Level Use

Most social work papers written for classes require the use of heading levels 1, 2, and sometimes 3, as illustrated in Table 5.2.

Table 5.2 Guide to Formatting Paragraph Headings

Level	Format
1	**Center Bold, Title Case Heading** Begin a new paragraph with a .5 space indention. Example: **My Summer Vacation** This past summer I spent my vacation time with my friends from school.
2	**Flush Left, Bold, Title Case Heading** Begin a new paragraph with a .5 space indention. Example: **Beach Vacation** This past summer, I spent my summertime off at the beach with my friends from school.
3	**Flush Left, Bold Italics, Title Case Heading** Begin a new paragraph with a .5 space indention (do not use italics in the text). Example: ***Surfing the Waves*** We brought our surfboards and used them every day.
4	**Indented, Bold, Title Case Heading, Ending with a Period.** Begin writing on the same line and continue as a regular paragraph. Example: **Beach Parties in the Evenings.** Every evening we met on the beach for an enjoyable get-together.
5	**Indented, Bold Italics, Title Case Heading, Ending with a Period.** Begin writing on the same line and continue as a regular paragraph. Example: ***Music, Singing, Dancing, and Story Telling.*** We had a great time and were sorry to see it come to an end.

Exercise 5.1

Working with a partner or on your own, review a written assignment previously submitted and graded with corrections written by the professor:

- If working with another student, trade assignments and make the corrections that were called for using the information in this chapter or from additional sources.
- If working alone, correct your assignment using information from this chapter and additional sources.
- Check citations and references, and run your paper through grammar and spelling software using Word, Grammarly, or Google Docs
- Check the headings to see if they comply with APA 7th Edition style.
- This exercise may take more than one sitting, so divide the work. For example, check spelling and grammar first, and then work your way through citations, references, and headings.

TABLES

If your paper requires you to construct a table with numbers or words, there are specific rules for their presentation. Before you begin creating tables, you may want to consider if a table is the best way to express your ideas. Often an outline using bullets can serve the same purpose and may be easier for the reader to navigate. If you want to use a table found in a published article or magazine, you may be able to copy and paste it into your paper, or take a screenshot of the table in print and add it to your work using the *Copy* and *Paste* function on your computer. If you do use a published table, be sure to give credit to the author. This is usually done by including the reference at the bottom of the table.

After considering the possibilities outlined above, if you still wish to create your own table, here is how to proceed.

Step 1

Go to the section on tables in the *APA 7th Edition Student Paper SetUp Guide* listed at the end of this chapter. There you will find illustrated instructions for creating different types of tables in APA 7th Edition style. It is best to find the easiest table to read for your purpose. Tables are meant to help the reader understand your work, not to make your ideas more complex than needed.

Step 2

Once you have identified the type of table you wish to use, begin the formatting using the *Table Setup* function on your word processor. You will be shown different styles to select from and will be asked for the number of rows and columns you need. Don't worry if you over or underestimate these numbers; you can always go back and add or subtract as required.

Step 3

Now that your table is set up, be sure the title describes the content. You will need to label tables by order of appearance in your paper: "Table 1," "Table 2," etc. You can see where to position the title and the table number by looking at the tables in this chapter.

EXAMPLE OF TABLE WITH MIXED WORDS AND NUMBERS

Our example presents a table that includes both words and numbers. As shown in the *Paper Setup Guide* section on tables, there are a variety of table types. It is best to select the one that is easiest to read, to help get your ideas across to the reader. Figure 5.1 is a screenshot taken from an article and is therefore listed as a figure.

ELEMENTS OF STYLE

Elements of style include the essential ways in which the APA 7th Edition guides your writing. Just about every aspect of APA 7th Edition formatting falls under the umbrella concept of "elements of style." Consult the *APA Student Paper Checklist* at the end of this chapter for instructions on and examples of almost every aspect of style you will need.

We also suggest you access the Perdue OWL *APA Formatting and Style Guide (7th Edition),* also listed at the end of this chapter. Both are excellent resources.

Table 5.3 Comparison of Means of Parenting Skills of Those Whose Children Were Placed in Out-of-Home Care and Those Who Were Not

Subscale	Family remained intact			Placement in out-of-home care		
	First Assessment mean (sd) [95%CI]	Final mean (sd) [95%CI]	d	First Assessment mean (sd) [95%CI]	Final mean (sd) [95%CI]	d
Overall safety	13.90 (3.91) [13.13–14.67]	15.43 (3.43) [14.76–16.10] *	0.42	13.56 (5.39) [9.41–17.70]	14.56 (5.57) [10.27–18.84] **	0.19
Parent-child interactions	12.55 (5.95) [11.40–13.69]	15.15 (7.00) [13.79–16.49] *	0.40	11.46 (7.07) [7.19–15.73]	11.69 (7.06) [7.42–15.96] **	0.03
Daily life skills	21.30 (5.67) [20.13–22.48]	25.80 (6.35) [24.49–27.11] *	0.75	16.80 (1.02) [13.97–19.63]	18.60 (5.59) [11.65–25.55] **	0.47
Total parenting	69.70 (14.25) [66.74–72.65]	79.58 (15.10) [76.45–82.70] *	0.68	44.80 (8.11) [34.74–54.86]	54.00 (11.44) [22.23–85.77] **	0.54

*$p < 0.001$; **$p > 0.05$ (n.s.)

Source: Adapted from: Zeitlin, W., Augsberger, A., Rao, T., Weisberg, D., & Toraif, N. (2021). Measuring parenting skills: Validating the Skills Assessment for Parents with Intellectual Disability. *Journal of Evidence-Based Social Work, 18*(2), 235–248. DOI: 10.1080/26408066.2020.1830909

On these websites, you will find guides to punctuation, spelling, capitalization, italics, abbreviations, numbers, statistics and mathematics, equations, and bulleted lists. Also included are page formatting, headings, fonts, and bias-free language.

BIAS-FREE LANGUAGE

Bias-free language is an element that warrants additional explanation because you do not want to unintentionally communicate prejudice, which is contrary to the values of most academic disciplines, including social work.

The writers of APA 7th Edition style are firm in their commitment to the use of bias-free writing. Here we present a partial list of the ones you are most likely to use. You will find a complete list of subjects covered in the *APA Online Guide to Bias-Free Language* on the website listed at the end of this chapter. This guide encompasses the areas of concern that experts have identified as sensitive to group bias practices.

Levels of Specificity

The concept of levels of specificity refers to language that avoids inaccurate generalizations that can communicate prejudice. An

example is the word "man" as an inclusive description of all people—
this is both inaccurate and potentially discriminatory. Instead, use
words such as "individuals," "people," or "persons." Additionally,
only mention specific characteristics of people if they are relevant to
your paper's topic. For example, if you are describing a group of
clients and one client has a different religion from the others, only
refer to that difference if it is important to your paper's topic. If you
did mention the difference in religious affiliation in this example,
you would need to describe the relevance of religious differences in
the group. Other examples include age (use an age range when
possible); disability (use specific types, such as "Alzheimer's," not
"dementia"); gender identity (only include when necessary and be
specific, such as "transgender man"); research (use "participants,"
"patients," or "clients"; not "people" or "children"); and racial or
ethnic groups (use "Chinese Americans," not "Asian Americans").
For sexual orientation, use "lesbians," "gay men," "bisexual people,"
or "heterosexual people" (not "gay" or "straight"); and for
socioeconomic status, use "below the federal poverty threshold" for
a family, not "low income" (APA, 2020, pp. 132–133).

Labels

Similar to specificity, by avoiding unnecessary labels, you can keep
your work free from biased language. Based on previous experiences
of derogatory name-calling, individuals and communities can be
sensitive to labels. It is best to find out how people wish to be
referred to, both individually and as a group. If you are working in
person, you can ask, noting that you wish to give the person the full
respect they deserve. If this is not possible, the internet may provide
a stopgap solution until you can make the necessary enquiries among
those involved. Here are a few basic tips that acknowledge people's
humanity. **Please note: these are general suggestions that may
change over time and may vary by region.**

- **Avoid using adjectives and nouns to label people:** Examples of what NOT to use include "the gays," "the poor," "drug
users," "the learning disabled," and "schizophrenics." When
writing about a person with a specific disability or disorder, use
"a person with schizophrenia" instead of a "schizophrenic," or

"a person with a learning disability." It may be acceptable to identify the disability first—such as when writing about "an autistic person." Deciding which to identify first, the person or the disability, depends on how people in the specific group define themselves. If you are not sure, ask for guidance either from a group member or from a knowledgeable person such as your supervisor or professor. Be respectful: When writing about factors such as age, gender, sexual orientation, and socioeconomic status, the most important strategy is to be respectful.

- **Age:** For individuals aged 12 years or younger, APA 7th Edition suggests the terms "infant," "child," "girl or boy," "transgender girl or boy," or "gender-fluid child." An individual aged 13 to 17 should be described as an "adolescent," "youth," "young woman," "young man," or "agender adolescent." Individuals aged 18 and older can be described using terms like "adult," "woman," "man," "transgender woman," "trans woman," "transgender man," or "trans man." Older adults are best referred to as "older adults." The word "senior" should be used only when referring to an organization title, such as a senior citizen organization. "Dementia" should be used instead of "senility."

- **Gender:** Use "men" and "women," not "males" and "females." Similarly, use "boys" and "girls"; and "transgender men" and "transgender women."

- **Sexual orientation:** This descriptor is best termed "sexual orientation," and not "sexual preference," or "sexual identity." The word "gay" can be used if it refers to both men and women. Use "gay man" and "gay woman," or in the latter case "lesbian," to differentiate between the genders. "LGBTQ+" should be used instead of "LGBT," as the latter term is less inclusive. It is best to avoid using the term "homosexuality" in most writing situations.

- **Socioeconomic status:** "Socioeconomic status" can be shortened to "SES" after the first use by including the acronym in parentheses: "socioeconomic status (SES)." Thereafter, you can simply use "SES."

- **Gender pronouns:** When preferred gender pronouns are not known, use "they," "them," and "theirs" for both individuals and groups.

- **Participation in social work treatment or research:** Use the term "client" in most cases. When working with multiple disciplines, such as on a research study with medical personnel, you can use the term "patients" or "consumers."

Bias-Free Language and Culture

You may have noticed that that bias-free language is connected to cultural norms. As culture is subject to change, what we think of as "bias-free" can also change. It is best to stay up to date in your writing to the best of your ability. By adhering to the examples in this volume and checking for other bias-free terms online—both with individuals and groups, and with your professors, as needed—you will be on safe ground for communicating respect and dignity.

If, for any reason, you mistakenly use a term in your assignment paper that may potentially offend a person or group, your professor may note the error and offer an alternative descriptor. If this occurs, it is best to thank your professor and state your intent to use bias-free language in future papers. Student errors of this type are common and can easily be fixed as long as social work values are followed.

Exercise 5.2

Working with a partner or on your own, consider how you could improve your use of labels, either in the past or currently. Consider your writing in terms of age, gender, sexual orientation, socioeconomic status, and participation in research or treatment:

- Using information in this chapter, how would you now describe people in these categories?
- If working with another student, critique each other. Where did you do well? What language might need correction?
- Write your corrections in a notebook or a computer file, along with the page number in this book where the correct attributions are listed.

CONCLUSION

In this chapter, we provide guidance on writing in APA 7th Edition style. In doing so, we combine the key elements of style found in the *APA Publication Manual, Seventh Edition* with online resources. This chapter is not meant to replace the *Manual* for students needing more details and writing options. The best way to use this chapter is to make a list of the information you need to complete your assignment. Once you have written the content, you will need to format your work in APA 7th Edition style—go ahead and do the best you can with what you already know. APA 7th Edition formatting should be the last task to take on in any writing project. Go through your drafted paper and ensure you have cited all quotations and paraphrases according to the information provided in this chapter. You may wish to consult online information using the suggested resources identified in the last section of this chapter. Finally, when your editing is complete, run the paper through a spelling and grammar software program once more. If you are satisfied that you have covered all bases, go ahead and submit!

Quick Tips: Writing Checklist

- Be sure to use citations throughout your paper, from first to last paragraph, as needed.
- The reference list should consist of only the references that were cited in your paper.
- Most people cannot remember all the rules for writing a reference list. Use software to create references in APA 7th Edition style or keep a book like this near your computer to look up the correct way to format references.
- Use headings for your writing. Refer to this book or online sources for the APA 7th Edition heading styles.
- Bias-free language is important for your writing. Refer to the section in this chapter or find instructions online using the sources listed below.
- Check out the sample paper using the link listed below and in Appendix A of this book for a visual example of a paper written in APA 7th Edition style.

FURTHER INFORMATION

Assistance with Grammar, Punctuation, Plagiarism and More

• Grammarly:
https://grammarly.com

Guidance on APA 7th Edition Style Writing

• The *APA 7th Edition Style Student Paper Setup Guide* has most of what you need to write APA 7th Edition style papers:
https://docs.google.com/viewer?url=https%3A%2F%2Fapastyle.apa.org%2Finstructional-aids%2Fstudent-paper-setup-guide.pdf
• The *APA Student Paper Checklist* reviews the areas of APA 7th Edition style in an easy-to-use checklist format:
https://apastyle.apa.org/instructional-aids/beginner-student-paper-checklist.pdf
• The *APA Style and Grammar Guidelines* provide links and information about formatting papers, in-text citations, mechanics of style, and bias-free language.
https://apastyle.apa.org/style-grammar-guidelines/
• The *APA 7th Edition Common Reference Examples Guide* also provides assistance in creating references:
https://apastyle.apa.org/instructional-aids/reference-examples.pdf
• The Perdue OWL *APA Formatting and Style Guide (7th Edition)* also addresses elements of style as well as formatting rules:
https://owl.purdue.edu/owl/research_and_citation/apa_style/apa_formatting_and_style_guide/index.html

Paper Example from Antioch University

• A paper example from Antioch University is included in Appendix A and can also be accessed at the following link:
https://docs.google.com/viewer?url=https%3A%2F%2Fwww.antioch.edu%2Fwp-content%2Fuploads%2F2019%2F12%2FAPA-7-Writing-in-APA-7th-Ed-Example-Paper.pdf

Reference Organizing and Citation Program Software

- Zotero organizes your references, searches websites and saves references for your future use:
  https://www.zotero.org
- EndNote assists in searching for references, organizes and stores references for future use, and creates citations and reference lists. School libraries subscribe to it and offer it to students:
  https://www.endnote.com
- Mendeley Cite creates citations and references as you write, and saves references for future use. It can be downloaded directly into your Word program. One word of caution: you need to use a Microsoft Word program from 2016 or later, and you may need to download it using Microsoft Edge as your browser:
  https://www.mendeley.com/reference-management/mendeley-cite

COMMON WRITING CHALLENGES

INTRODUCTION

This chapter provides perspectives on a variety of common writing challenges that many people experience. We addressed successful writing strategies in Chapter 1 and throughout this book. Here we will take a further look at the most common writing challenge for most students: beginning and continuing to write assignments. We will begin with a short review of the dimensions of writing procrastination and writing anxiety; and will then provide tips and suggest software that may help in overcoming them. Topics covered include the often-experienced difficulty of meeting deadlines and managing time. We will end with a brief statement about artificial intelligence (AI) programs.

OVERCOMING WRITING ANXIETY

First, let's clarify our use of a couple of terms. Writing anxiety is typically described as an emotional barrier to beginning to write or continuing once you start. "Procrastination" is defined as unnecessarily delaying or putting off doing something—in this case, writing. The difference between procrastinating and having writing anxiety is thought to be the emotional component present with anxiety; although it is likely that for many people, both are caused by a fear of writing. In this chapter, we will use the term "anxiety" for both, as it signifies the overall difficulty many students have in writing their assignments and submitting them on time.

There are many resources that describe the problem of writing anxiety and the steps in overcoming it. The one we think best

DOI: 10.4324/9781003168713-7

applies to social work students is *Symptoms and Cures for Writer's Block* by Perdue University's Online Writing Lab (OWL). We list this resource and others at the end of this chapter. One point stressed by the Perdue OWL help page is to remember that your initial draft can be changed. It is not a firm commitment. It's fine to put down ideas and then cut and paste, add and delete as needed. Once you get started, you may notice your anxiety about writing starts to decrease. Stick with it! The further you get in writing your assignment, the more confident you will feel, which will reduce your anxiety.

Here are tips to help beat writing anxiety!

Tip 1: Know Your Deadline

Assignment deadlines can cause anxiety and it is easy to put them aside when thinking about your daily activities. However, delaying strategies to avoid writing will only make things worse. Positive action is needed as a way of combating angst, even if it is just creating a plan for working on the assignment. The first step is to remain fully aware of your deadline so you can estimate both the time you will need and the time you have available to do the work. Most people underestimate the time needed to write an assignment, so it is a good idea to double your estimation. If there is time left over, you can celebrate your achievement.

Tip 2: Gather Your Ideas

As you are working out the time parameters, it is likely you will also be thinking about what to write. The writing process allows for the first two steps to be considered at the same time. Often, as you begin to think about the assignment, you may have a bunch of ideas, some useful and others far off track. One convenient feature of computers is the ease with which ideas can be moved around, sorted, and matched. As new ideas come to mind, they can be combined with earlier thoughts or added to the mix. You may find these additions help in eliminating what no longer relates to your overall writing theme. The amazing thing is that once words and phrases are in front of us, our brains start pulling them together and we begin constructing responses to the assignment.

Another useful technique is to begin the thought process by writing down ideas in a notebook. Simply writing ideas on paper helps to stimulate the thinking process. If you are not a paper notebook person, writing in a computer file may work for you. If you do use a computer, be sure to keep your work in a clearly labeled file—for example, "Assignment 2, Practice Class." That way, you will not need to spend time searching for work—time that you could use for other aspects of preparing your assignment.

Tip 3: Don't Dwell on the Past

Many students have experienced writing challenges and are concerned that these may reoccur. This can lead to wasted time; and it isn't logical, in the sense that we are constantly changing from our exposure to our environments. Negative thoughts are like fences that block the way to success. If this reflects how you feel in any way, stop in your tracks! It's time to break down the writing wall.

Tip 4: Believe in Yourself

If you think these tips have a psychological component, you are right. So much related to success in writing is also connected to how one views oneself. Questioning whether your ideas are relevant to the assignment is an aspect of self-doubt often attributed to writing anxiety. So how do you turn it around? Ideas for assignments are best anchored in what has previously been written on the topic. You can agree or disagree with published authors, as long as you know what they have presented in their work. Including your ideas as they apply to published studies is the best way to ensure you will be taken seriously. This is done by first describing and citing previous studies, and then commenting in your own words. It is important, though, to understand that comments related to cited studies are not necessary and should be included only when you need to express your opinion. Chapters 1 and 5 in this book provide information on how to use citations in the body of your paper and include a reference page at the end. Communicating your thoughts in professional social work language—a topic included in Chapter 2 and in the last section of Chapter 5—will further enhance your writing confidence.

Tip 5: Assess Your Work

Now that you are writing, it is up to you to assess how you are progressing. Your professor will ultimately assign your work a grade and offer comments, but the real evaluation is yours alone. Have you succeeded at your highest level, or could you have done better? How would you grade yourself: 100%, 90%, 80% of your ability? Don't be too hard on yourself. There is a saying to keep in mind when writing for assignments: "It's not a question of whether you will do well; rather, it is how well you will do."

MEETING DEADLINES AND TIME MANAGEMENT

One important challenge students often face in meeting writing deadlines is overcoming procrastination. This can be especially challenging for students who are concerned about their writing skills. Organizing your time, in general, is another challenge that may affect meeting deadlines. We address these challenges separately, providing suggestions for each to help writers overcome barriers that keep them from performing at their highest level.

Chapter 1 highlights the importance of meeting deadlines. We review and expand on this here by including time management as a skill that may present a variety of life challenges, including completing assignments. As you read through the following sections, consider which topics best reflect your experiences with writing; referring to resources on these topics will point you to dedicated information that can help you address those challenges.

Meeting Deadlines

Why are assignment deadlines so important? There are two main reasons:

- They are expected parameters to be met in professional social work tasks; and
- In the school setting, they help students and professors organize their writing work.

Let's start with the first reason: deadlines are expected to be met in professional social work settings. Missed deadlines can also have consequences for students in many areas, including applying for scholarships, grants, and other forms of financial aid. For your clients, missed deadlines can mean not receiving needed services. For your classes, your professors may reduce your grade if work is turned in late, which is a typical response to late assignments. Of course, sometimes they may waive a lateness penalty if you have a legitimate excuse, such as illness. Even so, it is best to avoid excuses whenever possible, because you do not wish to become known among your professors for often being late with assignments. This can and does happen.

Note that if you have a documented disability, you may be eligible for "reasonable accommodations." See your school's disabilities resource center to determine your eligibility.

The second reason for meeting deadlines is much more important for you, both personally and professionally. When you know the timeframe for completion of an assignment, and you take it seriously, it is far more likely that the assignment will get finished on time; you can then relax and enjoy your victory.

So, what are the hints and tips to help you meet deadlines? As we have noted, there are many websites that offer suggestions for meeting deadlines both in the business world and for students. All you need to do is use your search engine and select those that best resonate with you.

Here are some tips we have found online—although you may find others as well:

- **Estimate the time and resources you will need to complete the project:** We suggest writing these criteria in a notebook or an online file. You may find that at least some of these criteria can be used for many of your assignments. See Chapter 1 for more details on this.
- **Keep a calendar handy:** This allows you to visualize the days or weeks that you have to complete your work before the deadline. Visualizing time tends to force people to realistically appraise what they can do within the time allotted.
- **Break down your work into small units and establish a "to-do" list:** This reduces anxiety for some people, in that smaller tasks seem less onerous. An example of a small task on a to-do list would be to look for and collect references for your assignment from your online library. A file on your computer or dedicated flash drive can be used to store references and keep them ready to use.

- **Create a work schedule that allocates realistic time periods during which you will work on your assignment.** If you have multiple assignments, build them into the schedule as well. Your schedule may look like the one in Table 6.1, as an example. Tables can be as simple as this or more complex—the important point is that it works for you.

Table 6.1 presents an example schedule table that is easy to create.

Table 6.1 Work Schedule for This Week

Days	9AM-11AM	11 AM-12PM	1PM-3PM	3 PM-4PM	AFTER 4PM
Sunday	Break	Work On Assignment For Practice Class	Break	Work On Assignment For Policy Class	Work
Monday	Work	Break	Field	Field	Work
Tuesday	Class	Break	Class	Work	Work
Wednesday	Field	Field	Field	Field	Practice Assignment
Thursday	Class	Class	Library	Break	Policy Assignment
Friday	Field	Field	Field	Break	Practice & Policy Assignments Due by 12 Am
Saturday	Break	Work	Work	Break	Break

- **Stay positive:** Keeping to deadlines does not always come easily, although all improvements count toward your goal of ensuring on-time submissions. It may take a while, or it may happen quickly. In either case, you may be surprised at how good it feels to reach your deadline— especially if this is a challenge you have been struggling with for a long time.

Organizing Your Time

Let's get back to working with time. Organizing time is very similar to the concept of meeting deadlines, but there are some differences worth exploring further. Time organization—also called time management—is a concept that encompasses all your time, not just the time needed to devote to schoolwork. It takes the finite concept of time and places you in control of its use. One difference between the concepts of time organization and meeting deadlines is the idea of people prioritizing their time—that is, they allocate its use to whatever they think is most important. For students, this means deciding how much, when, and where time should be devoted to assignments, class attendance, fieldwork, and other school-related activities—concepts we mostly have addressed in this book. Additional aspects of time organization include decisions to accept external commitments to time, such as helping a friend move furniture or turning down such a request. We do not often think about our time as a resource to allocate as we choose. Of course, there are necessary time commitments we all have based on our family's needs, our own needs to care for ourselves, and the social expectations we all face. Having noted these likely additions, let's look at the bottom line: how do we choose to organize our time and how do our decisions affect our assignments?

To do this, we can look at our time resources first, followed by how we allocate our time:

- **Time resources are unique to each of us:** This means that we do not have equal resources left over after we put our time into absolute necessities including family obligations, financial pressures, and self-care. Additionally, our physical and emotional strengths play a role in time usage; as do cultural and religious expectations that are placed on many of us. When we look at these factors, it becomes clear that we have different amounts of time to devote to schoolwork. Our time-organizing skills need to be matched with our unique allocation of available time for school activities.
- **Prioritizing is crucial for effective time organization:** It may help to make a rank-ordered list of your time commitments. Create categories of commitments in a notebook or a computer file. Here are suggested examples: essential (time-fixed); necessary (time-flexible); occasional (may be postponed); and temporary (canceled). Once you have this visualized, you can assess how much time you can set aside for schoolwork.

- **Planning for effective time use is vital when school-based expectations pile up:** Sometimes it seems that your professors set assignment deadlines at the same time. This typically occurs during midterm and finals weeks. When this happens—and it does on occasion—you may need to temporarily change your regular time management schedule. Don't panic: an occasional change or rearrangement may be called for as a temporary solution. You may be surprised how understanding your family or employer will be, as long as you make up the time or give a date when you will return to your usual committed schedule.
- **Stay positive:** Don't get discouraged if your preparation plans are not working or if you are not following your own schedule for writing. Try a reset and give yourself credit for initiating the plan. If you miss a deadline for submitting an assignment, it is crucial to alert your professor and provide a realistic alternative date for its completion. It's always best to be proactive if you need additional time for assignments. Most professors will appreciate you taking the initiative by informing them of your expected late submission date.

RESOURCES FOR TIME MANAGEMENT

Many relevant websites can be accessed by searching for "time management skills for students" on your browser. Our favorite guide is posted on the Perdue OWL site and can be found at the end of this chapter. You may find others that are helpful as well. Please share your selections with class colleagues, friends, and even professors. They will appreciate your helpfulness with this common issue.

Another university-based web page specifically focused on time management, from Dartmouth University, may also be useful; again, this is listed at the end of this chapter.

Both of these websites can be accessed without charge. If you prefer books, here are three that appear to be focused on time management skills for college-level students and above:

- Stimmle, D. (2019). *Time management secrets for college students: The underground playbook for managing school, work, and fun.* College Success Academy Press.
- Douglas, A. (2021). *A student's guide to time management.* Independently published (available on Amazon).

- Sklar, M. (2014). *50 tips to help students succeed: Develop your student's time management and executive skills for life.* Aguanga.

Please note that we have not yet reviewed these books. We provide this list for your convenience only.

EXERCISES FOR LEARNING ABOUT AND IMPROVING WRITING ANXIETY AND TIME MANAGEMENT

- **Share your ideas:** Sharing your writing anxiety experiences and how you overcame them can help break down resistance to starting writing. Since most people have similar experiences, it is often helpful to tell a class colleague or friend about how you felt when you experienced writing anxiety. Feelings matter! After sharing your experiences, share how you were able to begin writing.
- **Map it out:** Look back at an assignment you successfully completed and retrace the steps you took to get it done. Identify each step, including the challenges and your pathways to working through them. By going through each step in this way, you can create a road-map for yourself and class colleagues with similar concerns.
- **Do the research:** By researching the experiences of well-known writers who overcame writing anxiety in the past, you can compare yourself with the "greats." You may take inspiration from learning that even successful writers sometimes find it difficult to write. You can begin by searching the internet for authors who have overcome writing anxiety by visiting https://lithub.com/is-it-real-25-famous-writers-on-writers-block/.

Exercise 6.1

You can do this exercise with a writing partner or on your own.

Many well-known writers have had their share of writing challenges. Search the web for information on how famous authors faced and overcame them. What can you learn from their experiences?

- You can begin by visiting *https://lithub.com/is-it-real-25-famous-writers-on-writers-block/*.
- Create web threads as you discover new information on the challenges faced by famous authors.
- Keep a notebook on your findings, so you can refer to it whenever you feel discouraged.

WRITING SOFTWARE

In addition to Microsoft Word and Google Docs, there are several types of writing software available, each with its own unique features. We described several of these in Chapter 5. *The Five Best Writing Apps for College Students* by Saint Leo University is very helpful (listed at the end of this chapter). Additionally, it is a good idea to check with your library if your university has purchased writing software for students and their recommendations for its use.

Other writing programs—such as Scrivener, FocusWriter, Write-Monkey, LibreOffice Writer, Scribus, and Author—are described in more detail on the TechRadar Pro website listed at the end of this chapter.

- **Tip:** When looking into writing programs, always check for grammar and spell check options. You also need to check if they are supported by PC (Windows) and Mac (macOS) operating systems. Also, as we describe in Chapter 5, several software programs have tiered options—for example, Grammarly Basic is offered with no fee, while Grammarly Premium has a fee attached. Your school librarian will know what you are entitled to use as part of your program fees.
- **Important note:** We all use the writing programs with which we feel most comfortable. However, these are not always compatible with the programs used by others, especially when some of us use Macs and some use PCs. When assignments are submitted by email as attachments, your professor may ask you to convert your work into a format that they can access. In most cases, this will be Word. This does not always happen; but when it does, writing

software programs other than Word have options to convert into Word format. Once you do the conversion, you should check for changes in the formatting of your document. In particular, look for spacing issues, most of which can be easily fixed.

AI SOFTWARE

By now, you will likely have heard much about AI. To learn more, it is best to search the internet for the latest information and products, as this field is evolving rapidly. Currently, you can use AI to improve your grammar and your word choices in much the same way as you can with Grammarly.

Products such as Microsoft's ChatGPT and Google's Bard can aggregate large amounts of available information by searching the internet; however, information that is not freely available is not included in the results, thus limiting its applicability in academic settings. AI products are not replacements for the human brain and are known to make errors or go completely off track with their answers. There is no doubt they will improve for future use; but it is difficult to imagine they will ever replace our thought processes, and thereby our writing, which synthesizes our unique thoughts with available information. There are also ethical and legal implications that need to be worked out as we move forward with AI technology. As these programs and others like them become more commonly used, we will hear from the leaders of the social work profession about the best way to use them. To keep up with the latest trends and your school's policy on the use of AI software, speak with a professor or your program director.

Exercise 6.2

You can do this exercise with a writing partner or on your own:

- Search the web for information on the pros and cons of using AI for student writing.
- If you are working with a writing partner, investigate and come up with a list of pros and cons for using AI writing software such as

ChatGPT or Bard. Consider its usefulness and harmfulness for social work writing.

- If you are working on your own, keep notes on the usefulness and harmfulness of these tools, being sure to revisit your list of pros and cons periodically.

One last comment on this subject: ultimately, you are responsible for your writing. Using software programs that offer to write your papers from scratch, using algorithms or computer-driven calculations that can aggregate data sets, may not be allowed by your school at this time. Find out how your program manages the use of AI.

CONCLUSION

Writing challenges include writing anxiety and difficulties organizing your ideas, setting aside the necessary amount of time to complete assignments, and prioritizing your time. We present useful ideas to overcome barriers that can impede your writing success. We also present examples of software that students sometimes find helpful in realizing the writing results they aspire to achieve.

Quick Tips: Writing Checklist

- Occasional occurrences of writing anxiety are common. Don't panic. Step away from your computer for a while, go for a run, meet a friend for coffee, or take time to relax. More often than not, temporary pauses from your work will refresh your mind, and you will find it easier to write when you return.
- Try using a daily schedule book with a section on tasks for the day. Then cross off each successful achievement, including writing assignments, to give yourself a visual victory.
- Pay attention to those red and blue lines that appear under words on your screen. Right click and make the suggested changes. Your writing will improve immediately.
- If you have been hesitant to use writing assistant software, try it out. You can always delete the results. Start with a program that's easy to use, such as Grammarly. You do not have to accept its suggestions, although you may find them useful.

FURTHER INFORMATION

General Writing Resources

- The Perdue OWL's *Symptoms and Cures for Writer's Block* has useful suggestions for overcoming writing anxiety, also known as "writer's block."
  https://owl.purdue.edu/owl/general_writing/the_writing_process/writers_block/index.html
- *Writing in Social Work* offers tips for writing for your social work assignments from Texas A&M University:
  https://www.tamuct.edu/coas/coas-special-topics/uwc/uwc-social-work.html#:~:text=Social%20Work%20writing%20needs%20to, based%20writing%20and%20scholarly%20writing.
- *Strengthening your Writing Skills: An Essential Task for Every Social Worker* is a four-page article by the National Association of Social Workers with useful information focused on improving social work writing skills:
  https://docs.google.com/viewer?url=https%3A%2F%2Fcareers.socialworkers.org%2Fdocuments%2FWritingSkillsLL.pdf
- Dalhousie University's *Writing Center Online Resource Guide* includes useful information and a sample social work paper with critical annotations:
  https://dal.ca.libguides.com/c.php?g=257176&p=1718037
- Social Work.org's *Writing Guide* addresses some of the issues which are covered in this book. You may find it useful as a review:
  https://www.socialwork.org/resources/writing-guide/
- Saint Leo University's *The Five Best Writing Apps for College Students* provides suggestions based on your style as a student:
  https://www.saintleo.edu/about/stories/blog/the-5-best-writing-apps-for-college-students
- Techrader Pro lists the lesser-used writing software programs on its website:
  https://www.techradar.com/best/free-writing-software

Time Management Resources

- Mindtools offers tips on organizing your time:
  https://www.mindtools.com/pages/article/meet-deadline.htm

- Keeping a "to-do" list plus other ideas are presented on the Hygger Project Management website:
  https://hygger.io/blog/11-tips-manage-time-improve-deadline-management-skills/
- Perdue University has a dedicated time management section on its website:
  https://www.purdueglobal.edu/blog/student-life/time-management-busy-college-students/
- Dartmouth University offers valuable guidance on time management for students:
  https://students.dartmouth.edu/academic-skills/learning-resources/time-management-tips

SKILLS IN SUPPORT OF CRITICAL WRITING

CRITICAL THINKING, CRITICAL READING, AND CRITICAL WRITING: LINKING ALL THREE

The concepts of critical thinking, reading, and writing are intricately linked in determining success in academic work. For the purposes of this chapter, we focus on writing as a critical outcome. By now, from reading this handbook, you will understand how important your writing is for communicating your ideas, getting good grades, and helping you achieve your career goals. Because critical writing focuses on critical thinking and reading skills, let's examine their meaning.

"Critical thinking" is defined as "the ability to engage in reflective and independent thinking" (lumen, n.d., p.1). It calls for actively assessing ideas and not automatically accepting everything you read in print or online. It requires you to use your own reasoning, which may be based on past learning, personal experiences, and analytical abilities. Please see the references section at the end of this chapter for additional information on critical thinking.

"Critical reading" refers to the process of reading to understand and evaluate the ideas presented. It calls on critical thinking processes to identify the authors' main points and evaluate them using your past learning and experiences. It may also encompass your own analysis and synthesis of the ideas presented. Critical reading considers the creation or reshaping of your own ideas based on connecting authors' thinking with your own. Please see the end of this chapter for additional resources on critical reading.

DOI: 10.4324/9781003168713-8

CRITICAL WRITING

Critical writing builds on the skills mentioned above; but in this case, you are also doing the writing. For your schoolwork, you need to consider two types of critical writing:

- writing to inform; and
- writing to react, apply, analyze, and synthesize (lumen, n.d.).

Writing to inform involves presenting information that is valuable to the reader. An example would be outlining the process and policies that an adoption agency uses to determine if prospective parents are suitable to adopt. In this example, you would describe the agency's process based on its policies and the step-by-step actions it takes to investigate prospective parents. If your assignment requires suggestions for changing the agency's adoption policies and processes, you would first inform the reader about its existing policies and then present your own responses and recommendations. The recommendations part of your paper may include your ideas based on examples from your research of how agencies with similar policies conduct their investigations. In other words, writing this paper involves an initial two-step process: first inform, then react. Your suggestions should be based on critical reading and thinking. For additional examples and information about writing papers for class, take another look at Chapter 1 of this book. Further resources are provided at the end of this chapter.

Before we move on, it's worth taking another look at critical reading as the bridge between critical thinking and critical writing. This is the essential link that connects the thought process with communicating your findings and the meanings you attribute to them.

CRITICAL READING

Social work education involves a lot of reading and writing assignments. In this section, we will give you some ideas on how to read effectively to improve your overall educational experience and, ultimately, communicate clearly what you have learned.

Social work students need to read different types of sources, including news articles, policy papers, textbooks, research articles, and practice articles. While there are differences in how easy or difficult these different texts are to read and understand, you will need to critically appraise everything you read.

Reading any type of educational material often introduces a new vocabulary. If you do not understand a word, guess its meaning, and then look it up! Were you right? To help make this task easier, we recommend downloading one of the many excellent dictionary apps onto your phone for easy access. Alternatively, you can enter the word into Google or another search engine and search for the definition.

As you read any source, consider answering the following questions in your own words:

1   What are the new ideas presented? What do you think about these ideas?
2   Are the ideas presented similar to or different from those in other sources? In what ways?
3   How do the ideas presented relate to your own experiences, either personally or professionally?
    •   If they are similar, how do the ideas in this source help you better understand your own experiences?
    •   If they are different, why do you think that is the case? What new ideas can you apply to your experiences?
4   Overall, what have you learned from this source?

Keep track of your responses so you can document what you learn from each source, as you will need to cite it in your assignments if you refer to it.

Below we provide helpful hints for reading different types of manuscripts, including textbooks, policy papers, research articles, and practice articles.

Textbook Reading

Typical reading assignments require you to read one or more chapters of a textbook. This can take quite a bit of time, so our first suggestion is to allow yourself enough time to get through each assignment.

We also recommend briefly previewing your textbook assignments before you begin reading. Look through the assigned chapter, taking time to read headings, look at tables, and evaluate illustrations. If you spend a few minutes on this task, you will get an overall sense of what each chapter is about. This can help set the stage for a more successful reading session.

When reading, tackle one section or subheading at a time, and then jot down your responses to the above questions for that section. By the time you finish a chapter, you should have done a lot of critical thinking and reflecting, and you will have meaningful notes to refer to later.

Reading Exercise 7.1

Working with a partner or on your own, use the following steps to critically read an assigned text:

- If you are working with a partner, read the same section of text and record your responses to the four questions related to critical reading. Compare and contrast your responses with those of your partner.
- If you are working on your own, read an entire assigned chapter and record your responses to the four questions related to critical reading for each section of the chapter. When you are finished with the chapter, review your responses to the questions for each section. Is there anything else that you want to recall about this chapter? If so, add it to your notes.

Reading Policy Papers

As a social work student, you will be asked to read and critique policies—that is, formal guidelines implemented by governments or organizations that state how things should be done. Government policies, for example, may be laws passed by federal, local, or state authorities to achieve a specific goal. Organizations such as social service agencies may have their own policies.

When reading policy papers, you should respond to the four questions identified above; but you should also pay attention to other considerations:

- Who are the authors, and why are they writing about a policy in this paper? Is it to propose something new? Does it meet a need? Is it a critique of an existing policy?
- Policy papers are often written to convince the reader of something. What are the authors of this paper trying to convince you of, and do they make a coherent case? That is, are they connecting the need for something to a law, regulation, or rule that would address that need? If there are holes in their arguments, make a note of them.

Reading Exercise 7.2

Working with a partner or on your own, use the following steps to critically read an assigned policy paper:

- If you are working with a partner, read the same paper and record your responses to the four questions above related to critical reading. Additionally, comment on the two considerations for the analysis of policy papers listed above. Compare and contrast your responses with those of your partner.
- If you are working on your own, read an assigned policy paper and record your responses to the four questions related to critical reading. Additionally, comment on the two considerations for the analysis of policy papers listed above. Review your notes. Is there anything else that you want to recall about this paper later? If so, add it to your notes.

Reading Research Articles

During your career as a social work student, you will need to read research articles. Research articles differ from the other types of reading we have described previously because they often contain terminology related to the research itself that may be unfamiliar to social work students. As a result, students often fall into the trap of only reading the abstract—a brief summary of the research presented at the beginning of the article—and not reading the rest of the paper, which contains important information.

Before we launch into tips about how to effectively read research articles, we want to give you some good news! Almost all research articles are structured the same way, so you can use this to your advantage. In addition to the abstract, research articles typically contain five sections that are introduced with headings:

- **Introduction:** This section explains the overarching problem that the article is trying to address. It explains why the research has been conducted and, in the literature review, it summarizes what has been studied in the past to address the overarching problem. Finally, the last paragraph of this section usually describes the purpose of the study that is being presented.
- **Methods:** This section is effectively the "recipe" of the research article. Like any good recipe, it lists the ingredients; in a research article, these include the *who*, *what*, *when*, and *where* of the study. That is, this section explains *who* was included in the study; *what* was evaluated or measured; and *when* and *where* the study took place. Continuing with the recipe analogy, the methods section explains *how* the research was conducted in detail. That is, once you have the ingredients, the methods section tells you what was done with those ingredients to complete the research.
- **Results:** This is often the hardest section for students to understand because it may contain a lot of numbers, charts, tables, and research jargon. This section tells the reader what the researchers found, but with no interpretation: it's "just the facts."
- **Discussion:** This section contextualizes the results and generally includes less technical terminology than the results section. Here, you should find what the study means to social work practice, policy, or education. The authors will also describe the limitations of the study (even the best research studies have them), and what the authors think should be done next. This section also contains concluding remarks.
- **References:** This section lists all the works that were cited in the body of the article. While you may not read this section, it can be used to find additional articles on the topic.

We recommend you start by reading the introduction to any research article you are assigned or that you look for on your own. Consider the overall problem that the article addresses and which aspects of it the authors are studying. If the article remains relevant to your interests or assignment, continue reading. If not, you may want to look for something else.

Next, read the methods section. Who were the research participants? To what degree are they similar or different from your clients and the issues they face? The more similar the participants are to your clients' context, the more relevant the findings will be to your work as a social work student.

For a quick overview, you may want to read the introduction first and then skip to the discussion section, while considering the relevance of the study to your own work. An additional step would be to specifically identify the research questions, sometimes noted as the purpose of the study which is found at the end of the introduction. If those research questions are relevant to you, move to the discussion to see how the authors handled their response to the questions they posed. The discussion section should articulate the study's contribution to the social work profession and to you as a student.

Finally, and as a review, we suggest you reread the abstract. Does it help you understand your response to the four questions that should be addressed in every reading assignment? If something is missing, you might want to make a note of that too.

Reading Exercise 7.3

Working with a partner or on your own, use these steps to critically read an assigned research article:

- If you are working with a partner, read the same article and record your responses to the four questions related to critical reading. Additionally, explain the overarching problem the study was conducted to address, what the researchers found, and the relevance of those findings to social work. Compare and contrast your responses with those of your partner.
- If you are working on your own, record your responses to the four questions related to critical reading. Additionally, explain the overarching problem the study was conducted to address, what the researchers found, and the relevance of those findings to social work. After reading the abstract, how similar or different from the abstract are your notes? Is there anything else that you want to recall about this paper later? If so, add it to your notes.

Reading Social Work Practice Articles

You can easily apply the four questions listed above when reading practice articles. Practice articles typically begin with an abstract that describes the purpose and the practice method, usually in terms of how clients met (e.g., individually, in groups, in person, or virtually). It may also include the treatment theory (e.g., cognitive behavioral or psychodynamic therapy). Finally, the author(s) may note relevant information about the participants, which may include their shared social or economic problems, their environments, and—if the article relates to diagnosed clients—their past or current symptoms and levels of functioning.

Students often use practice articles to affirm the work they are presenting about their own clients. This makes it especially important to read practice articles carefully to be sure they address your work, in terms of either the practice method, the clients' personal or environmental stressors, or the outcomes of their described interventions. In other words, is there a fit between your work and that described in the article? If not, it is better to find another article.

What happens if there is a fit in terms of the participants, but not in terms of the interventions or how the clients met? Is the article still useful for you? It may still have relevance as an example of a different way of working with clients like yours, or if there is an aspect of the work that is similar to yours. Reading practice articles carefully can make the difference between affirming your work, or the opposite—showing what could be interpreted as a better way.

Reading Exercise 7.4

Working with a partner or on your own, use the following steps to critically read an assigned practice article:

- If you are working with a partner, read the same practice paper and record your responses to the four questions related to critical reading. Additionally, explain how the elements of practice in the article were conducted, including the participants' overall shared problems, the practice method, and the theory. Address the practice outcome(s) and the relevance to social work. Compare and contrast your responses with those of your partner.

- If you are working on your own, read an assigned practice paper and record your responses to the four questions related to critical reading. Additionally, explain how the elements of practice in the article study were conducted, including the participants' overall shared problems, the practice method, and the theory. Address the practice outcome(s) and the relevance to social work. After reading the paper, how similar to or different from the abstract and the paper are your notes? Is there anything else that you want to recall about this paper later? If so, add it to your notes.

CRITICAL WRITING CAN BE INFORMATIVE, REACTIVE, AND CREATIVE

Critical writing follows critical reading in the sequence we describe in this chapter. At the beginning of the chapter, we discussed the two essential elements of critical writing: being informative and being reactive. To reiterate, a typical social work assignment paper contains sections that are informative, sections that are reactive, and possibly sections that are mixed. You may first describe a social work-related policy, practice situation, or research finding. In sequence, you may then react with material from your practice experience or from what you have read. You can move from informing to reacting and back again as many times as makes sense, provided that the paper flows smoothly. Please refer to Chapter 1 for additional guidance and examples on writing assignment papers.

Writing creative social work papers doesn't mean including a poem or song lyrics, or drafting an essay based on a fictionalized subject. It can, however, involve writing about a topic from a different perspective than what you have previously read on a subject. Fiction writers use this skill to enhance drama and interest in their subject. They switch perspectives from one character to another as they move along the storyline. Character A describes an aspect of the plot in one chapter, which may be followed by Character B's point of view in the next. This keeps the reader interested and engaged, and can provide greater depth to the experiences of A and B by creating a new perspective: A + B.

Can this technique be applied to social work writing? If so, how, and what advantage might possibly be achieved? Let's look at a practice assignment where you might be describing an interaction with a client. We can use the formula: writing to inform + writing to react.

At the beginning of the assignment, you inform the reader of the reason for the interaction by providing the psychosocial information that is the basis of your work with the client. This may include the client's history related to their presenting problem and the work you have both completed so far.

Moving forward, you now switch to the reaction phase of the assignment. Typically, you might describe the rationale driving your social worker/client interactions. You might describe the successes and challenges that have accompanied your work, including your personal reactions to both. Then you go on to outline your thinking on next steps to enhance the client's progress—backed up, of course, with citations for the references you used. Once you have added an introduction and a summary, and are certain that you have responded to the assignment requirements, you will have a perfectly fine format for a practice assignment paper.

Adding Creativity by Using Multiple Perspectives

The multiple perspective format brings both the client's thoughts and yours closer to the reader by shifting back and forth from third-person description to first-person ideation. This can be constructed by including short transcripts of social worker/client interactions followed by your interpretation of their significance. This format requires you to keep the transcripts short and your interpretations focused. If the transcripts are longer than a sentence or two, you risk distracting the reader from the purpose of the paper. Similarly, if your interpretations are overly long (i.e., more than a few sentences), you may risk undermining the interesting aspect of the method.

Sometimes the transcripts are called "voices"—meaning the voices of the client and the social worker. You may want to try this technique out in a few sections of a paper to see how it works for you. One important point to keep in mind: do not confuse this technique with your process recordings (although you may use material extracted from process recordings in applying this technique). The idea here is to demonstrate how the interactions between the client and the social worker relate to the paper's purpose, which is usually stated at the beginning of the assignment.

The "How-To" Paper

Social work papers are fine in the typical format described above and in Chapter 1. Nonetheless, if you can rationalize the fit, you might want to add a section to your assignment paper that explains how you went about engaging or intervening with a client. By providing an example of your work that you regard as successful, you are indirectly highlighting your competence as a social worker. For this type of interaction, you can use a transcript or a descriptive narrative. Again, keep the example short—you do not want to confuse your work on the paper with your process recordings.

Additional Creative Suggestions

The examples of creative social work writing discussed above primarily relate to practice papers. For policy and research papers, you may want to use media infusions. Photos, videos, voice recordings, and screenshots can add interest to your assignment papers if their inclusion is allowed. IMPORTANT: **do not** take photos of clients, even if you have their permission. There are very few exceptions to this rule; but for the most part, you may not violate client confidentiality and privacy. Don't focus on exceptions because rules change, and you do not want to be caught off guard with a photo you took a while ago that is now unacceptable. You may, with permission, take photos of neighborhoods, agency professionals, and school colleagues. The same rules apply to voice and video recordings. Proceed with care on these as well, and do not use them in any published format without written consent.

WRITING AS A PROFESSIONAL SOCIAL WORKER: WRITING REPORTS

Social work report writing differs from writing for classes in that it focuses on facts and requires that important information be positioned at the very beginning of the social work report. If anchors are provided, as is the case with many forms, social workers are often required to use them. Examples of anchors include name, age, presenting problem, current functioning, diagnosis (if any), and living arrangements. If there is no outline provided, you should write about the client system in a fact-filled, efficient style. Essentially, thinking about our formula of "inform + react," writing about clients should be heavily weighted toward the "inform" side. There may be room to add your personal assessment of the client system at the end of the report. Here is an example of a client referral without anchors.

Example of a Freestyle Written Client Referral

Joan Smith is a 23-year-old single mother living with her six-month-old male child, her mother, and her stepfather in a small apartment in Chicago's South Side after hospitalization. She currently needs housing and reports her current living conditions as crowded and "unfriendly." She came to the Acme Agency in June 2023 complaining of feeling hopeless and sad most of the day, and was given a preliminary diagnosis of major depression, single episode, moderate. She denies use of substances including alcohol. Ms. Smith has a very limited relationship with the child's father, who is currently a full-time student with few financial resources. She presents no known risks: She denies suicidal ideation, has no previous violent behavior, and is actively caring for her child. Her judgment is assessed as good.

Ms. Smith is well regarded, and I see her as someone who can adjust to a new housing environment.

In this example, only the last sentence is reactive, while the rest of the referral is informative. The diagnosis is not cited because it is commonly used and is immediately recognized by social work professionals.

Additional information and suggestions for professional writing can be found in Chapter 2 of this book. Consult with your professor and your internship supervisor for writing suggestions. Finally, your school may have a guide on writing for the social work profession. If so, follow its instructions as your primary source for writing, and use this book as an informative enhancement.

Writing Exercise 7.5

Working with a partner or on your own, write a brief client referral based on the example shown above. Be sure to use the inform + react formula in your referral.

- If you are working with a partner, decide on the essential details needed for a referral to an agency for social work services and concrete services after hospitalization. Agree on the reason for a client's hospitalization, their environmental resources, and any special needs they may have. Your primary goal is to write a referral for services that will help keep the client from returning to the hospital. Write the referral independently, and compare and contrast your work with your partner's.

- If you are working on your own, decide on the essential details needed for a referral to an agency for social work services and concrete services after hospitalization. Consider the reason for the client's hospitalization, their environmental resources, and any special needs they may have. Your primary goal is to write a referral for services that will help keep the client from returning to the hospital. Write the referral and compare it with the one written in this chapter. How is yours similar or different? Consider a rationale for the way you have written the referral.

CONCLUSION

In this chapter, we examine the link between critical thinking, reading, and writing, with the goal of enhancing your social work writing skills. We identify four questions for you to consider when reading an article, to help guide your critical reading and thinking:

- What new ideas for you are presented in the article?
- Are these ideas similar or different from those in other sources you have read?
- How do the new ideas relate to your own experiences?
- Overall, what have you learned from this source?

Critical writing focuses on two distinct aspects of a social work assignment paper: writing to inform and writing to react. While you can move from inform to react and back again throughout an assignment, the distinction should be made clear to the reader.

We provide a brief description of how social work writing can be creative as well as informative and reactive. Finally, writing as a social work professional is illustrated, with an example of a client referral.

Quick Tips: Critical Thinking, Reading, and Writing

- Spend time reading and responding to the four questions related to critical reading. This will build critical thinking skills while providing you with useful notes that you can refer to later.
- Identify the parts of your writing that inform and react. Are they separate? If not, then rearrange.
- Creative social work writing must pay attention to rules and client privacy. Stay within the bounds of rules when using cameras, voice recordings, etc.

FURTHER INFORMATION

Building Skills

- This free course by lumen provides in-depth information on critical thinking, reading, and writing. For students who find that they would like extra support in reading difficult material, this site offers multiple examples, videos, and exercises to support college students at all levels:
  https://courses.lumenlearning.com/suny-esc-introtocollegereadingandwriting/chapter/introduction-critical-reading-writing/
- The University of North Carolina at Chapel Hill provides useful tips on taking notes while reading. It presents a number of methods based on the way students learn and the format of text (electronic vs. print). It also suggests app-based note-taking programs that help students organize their thoughts:
  https://learningcenter.unc.edu/tips-and-tools/taking-notes-while-reading/

- Cornell College in Mount Vernon, Iowa has tips for reading textbooks. These tips help with time management, note-taking, and critical comprehension, and promote active reading: https://www.cornellcollege.edu/student-success-center/academic-support/study-tips/reading-textbooks.shtml
- Dr. Amina Yonis created a creating an interesting video on reading research papers effectively. She promotes similar methods for reading research articles as we do, and she illustrates them well: https://www.youtube.com/watch?v=Gv5ku0eoY6k
- Political Science Guide provides basic information on policy papers, including what they are and what they entail. This site also provides links to sample policy papers and additional resources for effectively writing policy papers and reports: https://politicalscienceguide.com/home/policy-paper/
- This article presents a creative way of presenting case studies using a collaboration model:
    Boxall, K., McKenzie, V., Henderson, G., Aishath, S., & Mazza, D. (2018). Reimagining social work case studies: A social work—creative writing collaboration. *Social Work Education, 37*(7). 881–894. https://doi.org/10.1080/02615479.2018.1458831

APPENDIX A
EXAMPLE OF A WELL-WRITTEN PAPER

Source:

Retrieved from:
https://www.antioch.edu/wp-content/uploads/2019/12/APA-7-Writing-in-APA-7th-Ed-Example-Paper.pdf

Appendix A has been directly reproduced from the original source with permission from Antioch University, Santa Barbara Writing Center.

Change from APA 6: No Running head

Every page has a page number in the header

Student Paper Example
Based on the Seventh Ed. of *the
Publication Manual of the American
Psychological Association*

Title in bold, Capitalize All of the Major Words; no word limit.

Writing in APA Style 7th Edition Example Paper

Use same font size for everything in the entire document

Student Name

One blank double-spaced line under title.

Antioch University Santa Barbara

Course Name

Instructor Name

Student Name, Institution, Course Name & Number, Instructor, and Due Date, all on separate lines

January 8, 2020

Entire document should be double-spaced.

APA 7 no longer requires 12-pt. Times New Roman.

Permitted fonts:
- 12-pt. Times New Roman
- 11-pt. Georgia
- 11-pt. Calibri
- 11-pt. Arial
- 10-pt. Lucida Sans

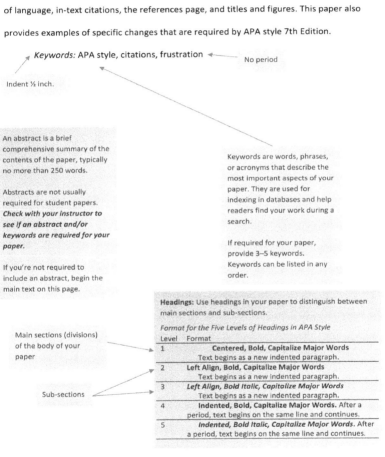

Page number

1 inch margin

Abstract ◄———— Level 1 heading
(see box below)

This paper describes some basic parts of writing in APA style 7th Edition. These components include seven major areas: the title page, abstract, formatting concerns for student writing, use of language, in-text citations, the references page, and titles and figures. This paper also provides examples of specific changes that are required by APA style 7th Edition.

Keywords: APA style, citations, frustration ◄———— No period

Indent ½ inch.

An abstract is a brief comprehensive summary of the contents of the paper, typically no more than 250 words.

Abstracts are not usually required for student papers. *Check with your instructor to see if an abstract and/or keywords are required for your paper.*

If you're not required to include an abstract, begin the main text on this page.

Keywords are words, phrases, or acronyms that describe the most important aspects of your paper. They are used for indexing in databases and help readers find your work during a search.

If required for your paper, provide 3–5 keywords. Keywords can be listed in any order.

Headings: Use headings in your paper to distinguish between main sections and sub-sections.

Format for the Five Levels of Headings in APA Style

Level	Format
1	**Centered, Bold, Capitalize Major Words** Text begins as a new indented paragraph.
2	**Left Align, Bold, Capitalize Major Words** Text begins as a new indented paragraph.
3	***Left Align, Bold Italic, Capitalize Major Words*** Text begins as a new indented paragraph.
4	**Indented, Bold, Capitalize Major Words.** After a period, text begins on the same line and continues.
5	***Indented, Bold Italic, Capitalize Major Words.*** After a period, text begins on the same line and continues.

Main sections (divisions) of the body of your paper

Sub-sections

Title is bolded and
centered, Capitalize
All of the Major Words

Repeat title from Title page

Writing in APA Style 7th Edition Example Paper

Level 1 heading
(see p. 2)

Writing in the style of the American Psychological Association (APA) is a regular practice

for students of higher degree programs in psychology and many programs in science. The new

edition of the manual has made several changes, such as endorsing the use of the singular *they*,

as exemplified in the next sentence. Each student writer who applies the new APA student

writing standards may encounter different challenges, however, they may use the resources

Use singular
"they"

provided by the AUSB Writing Center for support in learning the relevant new rules.

According to the seventh edition of the *Publication Manual of the American*

Psychological Association (2019), the style's broad applicability "helps authors present their

ideas in a clear, concise, and organized manner" that "uniformity and consistency enables

1 inch
margins on
all sides

readers to (a) focus on the ideas being presented rather than formatting and (b) scan works

quickly for key points" (p. xvii). Since this paper is mostly written in the seventh edition of APA

style, attentive readers will note that it has many examples of changes from the sixth edition.

One
space
after a
period

Most of the rules demonstrated here are those a student will need to have some acquaintance

with in order to write easily according to the student writing guidelines, which are distinct from

APA's new journal article reporting standards (Paiz et al., 2013).

New in APA 7:
Use "et al." for three
or more authors

Level 1 heading
(a main section)

The Structure of a Paper in APA Style

The APA style guidelines are designed for primary research papers that usually contain

the following sections: (a) introduction, (b) method, (c) results, (d) discussion, and (e)

references. However, the actual headings may vary depending on the type of paper one is

writing (American Psychological Association, 2019). For example, papers that do not describe

primary research or original experimental data may omit the method, results, and discussion sections (Xyers, Young, Zucherman, & Anne, 2019, p. 291). Some sections may be broken into

subsections, in which case the authors must use the appropriate headings and subheadings

(Xyers, Young, Zucherman, & Roberts, 2019, para. 4).

Exception to "et al." rule for 3 or more authors: Include as many authors as needed to distinguish between sources with the same first author(s).

Organizing the Main Body

Level 2 heading (a sub-section)

Most APA style papers written by students are not experimental; the organization of

headings and subheadings within the main body of the paper is therefore particularly

important. In certain cases, the author might use additional major sections, such as a literature

review, to introduce their own material.

Level 3 heading (a sub-section of the Level 2 sub-section)

Organizing the Main Body When There are Additional Content Concerns

Short papers usually only need Level 1 and 2 headings

In some common graduate assignments, students are instructed to compare therapeutic

models, provide possible interventions given specific presenting problems, or engage in case

study analyses. These papers may have particular sections (such as presenting problem, or

socio-cultural considerations of a given model).

Level 4 heading (see p. 2)

Language Concerns in the Body of the Paper. Sometimes, writers who are just

becoming comfortable with APA style, or with academic writing in general, will mimic academic

language in ways subtly less clear than writers who use academic register fluently. For example,

one might write the following sentence, which sounds academic to the mental ear, but in which

almost everything is done poorly:

If a quotation is 40 words or more, use a block quote format: new line, indent ½ inch, double space, no quotation marks.

> during the preparatory process of elucidating the critical and fundamental elemen[t]
>
> this theory for analysis, it would be observed that certain subjective elements of t[he]
>
> theory would be excessively situational to the point of being non-applicable outsid[e]
>
> the theorists' particular circumstances. (Goodwin, 2012a)

For block quotes, period comes before citation.

We observe that such a sentence serves little use beyond parody. The same sentiment can be

expressed in appropriate academic register in the following fashion: this theory is based on

subjective components and thus is not widely applicable (Goodwin, 2012b).

2 Styles of In-text Citations: Narrative & Parenthetical:

Level 4 heading → **Language Concerns as Issues of Unstated Academic Expectation.** Writers for whom the

distinction between the two earlier examples is unintuitive should not be dismayed. Graham

Narrative citation style

and Harris (1997) have shown that an academic style of writing is slowly learned, and is not

Para-phrase often intuitive. Often, the rules of academic English, and American academic English in

Parenthetical citation style

particular, are presented as assumptions rather than with explicit guidance (Graham & Harris,

1997). A student may look at their peers and see no one else asking questions about unclear

elements of an assignment, or unclear expectations, and try to muddle through on their own

No page # (see box below) rather than raising the issue. However, most academic expectations need to be explicitly taught

at some point, so students should not feel bad asking for clarification. Often, if one writer has a

question about the expectations, many others do also (S. Harter, personal communication,

September 30, 2018). ← Personal communication formatting example. Cite in text but not on References page. (see p. 7)

Level 1 heading → **In-Text Citations and References**

The American Psychological Association (APA) encourages authors to cite any works

that have impacted their own (APA, 2019). In general, the style guide recommends

paraphrasing sources rather than using too many direct quotes, "because paraphrasing

Cite the specific page number of direct quotes.

allows you to fit material to the context of your paper and writing style" (APA, 2019, p. 270).

A direct quote is best employed when the original author has stated a point particular

memorably, concisely, or effectively, or when the original author is providing a technical

About page numbers:
- Use for direct quotes
- Use for paraphrases of *information on a specific page*
  - Otherwise, optional for paraphrases

definition or explanation of a term. Under other circumstances, a paraphrase is usually more efficient than a direct quotation. Both paraphrased ideas as well as quotations need to be cited, though; only common knowledge does not require a citation. A good general rule of thumb might be: "when in doubt, cite it, and if you don't have a citation, double-check" (S. Chase, personal communication, August 12, 2017). ← Personal communication formatting example. Cite in text but not on References page. (see p. 7)

Writers using APA style should be careful to format their citations appropriately. Most in-text citations follow the format of author and year in parentheses, providing page numbers (or paragraph numbers) for every direct quotation. For paraphrases/summaries in your own words, include a page number when information is from a specific page of a source; otherwise a page number is optional, but may be helpful. The formatting of references in the references list, however, is more complicated, and writers should check their work to ensure that they have used the appropriate format for each citation, depending on the type of source.

Figures and Tables

As shown in Table 1, the seventh edition of APA has made some changes to the formatting of figures and tables. For example, figures now use the same title format as tables (see Figure 1). ← Use table and figure numbers to refer the reader to tables and figures. Do not write "see the table above/below".

Final Recommendations

APA style is an effective way of formatting and presenting complex material. APA can be time-consuming to learn; visit us in the AUSB Writing Center for help with any of your APA questions.

References should be in
alphabetical order and
double spaced.

Level 1 heading

References

American Psychological Association. (2019). *Publication manual of the American Psychological*

Association (7th ed.). ← When publisher & author are the same, omit that info.

Goodwin, J. (2012a). Made up examples of bad academic writing. *Academic Writing, 343*(1),

Same author,
same year:
use a & b

1006–1010. http://doi.org/11.1136/acadbad.12345 ← Include DOI as
hyperlinked URL

Capitalize only
the first word
of a journal
article and
subtitle.

Goodwin, J. (2012b). Good reading is hard writing: Another made-up journal article about

academic writing. *Reading & Writing,* 25(3), 143–152.

http://doi.org/10.1234/readwrite.123456789

Graham, S., & Harris, K. R. (1997). It can be taught, but it does not develop naturally: Myths and

realities in writing instruction. *School Psychology Review, 26*(6), 414–424.

Include
up to 20
authors

Paiz, J. M., Angeli, E., Wagner, J., Lawrick, E., Moore, K., Anderson, G., Franks, M., Paul, R.,

Keech, E., Ruiz, G., Allison, A., Caterelli, B., Zhou, M., Soong, R., Nguyen, Y., Bedo, O.,

Use a
hanging
indent

Sanders, B., Howard, C., Denny, H., ... Keck, R. (2013). Online writing: The challenges of

learning APA. *Journal of Psychotherapy.* http://doi.org/10.4567/apa-style.67810

Xyers, K., Young, G., Zucherman, F., and Anne, A. (2019). Example with multiple authors. In G. Y.

Iwamasa & P. A. Hays (Eds.), *Big Book of Examples* (2nd ed., pp. 287–314). CRC Press.

Xyers, K., Young, G., Zucherman, F., and Roberts, B. (2019, June 1). *Example citation for multiple*

authors. BBC News. http://www.bbcnews.com/example-for-multiple-authors.html

The References provides the information necessary for a reader to
locate and retrieve any source you cite.
• *Every source* you cite must appear on your References page.
• References page *only* includes sources cited in the body of your paper.

New in APA 7:
- No place of publication for books
- Leave hyperlinks
- Do not use "retrieved from" or a retrieval date unless the website content updates often by design (e.g., social media)

Exception: Do not include personal
communication on your References
page, e.g., emails or interviews, since
they are not recoverable. Instead,
cite them in-text. (See p. 6.)

Table 1

An Example of an APA Style Table

Limited shading and borders now preferred. (Do not use vertical borders to separate data.)

Table or Figure	Change from 6th Edition
Table	Mostly the same for simple tables, but avoid unnecessary borders or shading in a table
Figure	Now uses same title format as tables

Note. A table note may optionally be included under the table to clarify the contents of the table for the readers of the manuscript.

Figures and tables are left-aligned

Place each table on a separate page, followed by each figure on a separate page

Figure 1

Writing in APA Style

Figure titles now parallel to table titles (above the figure)

Note. A figure note may optionally be included under the figure to clarify the contents of the figure for the readers of the manuscript.

APPENDIX B
COMMONLY USED ACRONYMS
Adapted from *Glossary of Acronyms and Abbreviations*

Source:

https://www.state.nj.us/humanservices/resources/acronyms.html

A

AAA	Area Agency on Aging
AADSP	Alzheimer's Adult Day Services Program
AATOD	American Association for the Treatment of Opioid Dependence
ACL	Administration for Community Living
ACLU	American Civil Liberties Union
ACSA	AGIS (AssistGuide Information System) County SAMS Administrator
ADA	Americans with Disabilities Act
ADADS	Alcohol and Drug Abuse Data System
ADD	Attention Deficit Disorder
ADHD	Attention Deficit Hyperactivity Disorder
ADC	Adult Day Care
ADL	Activities of Daily Living
ADL(s)	Activity (Activities) of Daily Living
AFC	Adult Family Care
AHCPR	Agency for Health Care Policy and Research
AIDS	Acquired Immune Deficiency Syndrome
AL	Assisted Living
ALD	Assistive Listening Device
ALF	Assisted Living Facility
ALP	Assisted Living Program
ALR	Assisted Living Residence
ALS	Amyotrophic Lateral Sclerosis (a.k.a. Lou Gehrig's Disease)
AMTA	American Methadone Treatment Association
AO	Administrative Order
AoA	Administration on Aging
AOC	Administrative Office of the Courts
AOD	Alcohol and Other Drugs
APC	Area Plan Contract
APS	Adult Protective Services
ARRA	American Recovery and Reinvestment Act of 2009

ASAA	American Society of American Addictions
ASAM	American Society of Addiction Medicine
ASI	Addiction Severity Index
ASL	American Sign Language
ATTC	Addiction Technology Transfer Center

B

| **BSS** | Board of Social Services (also known as County Welfare Agencies) |
| **BVI** | Blind and Visually Impaired |

C

CADC	Certified Alcohol and Drug Counselor
CAP	Consumer Assistance Program
CARF	Commission on Accreditation of Rehabilitation Facilities or Council on Accreditation of Residential Facilities
CART	Communication Assisted Realtime Translation
CBOSS	County Boards of Social Services
CBT	Cognitive Behavioral Therapy
CCR	Community Care Residence
CCRC	Continuing Care Retirement Communities
CCW	Community Care Waiver
CD	Chemical Dependence or Chemically Dependent
CDC or **CDCP**	Centers for Disease Control and Prevention
CDS	Controlled Dangerous Substance
CDSMP	Chronic Disease Self-Management Program
CFR	Code of Federal Regulations
CFSR	Child Family Service Review
CFT	Child Family Team
CHIP	Children's Health Insurance Program
CHSP	Congregate Housing Services Program
CIACC	County Interagency Coordinating Council
CIL	Center for Independent Living

CIMU	Critical Incident Management Unit
CLP	Community Living Program
CMO	Care Management Organization
CMS	Centers for Medicare and Medicaid Services or Contract Management System
CN	Certificate of Need
CNA	Certified Nursing Assistant
COSA	Children of Substance Abusers
CP	Cerebral Palsy
CPCH	Comprehensive Personal Care Home
CPS	Child Protection Specialist or Case Practice Specialist
CQI	Continuous Quality Improvement
CST	Child Study Team
CWA	County Welfare Agency
CWLA	Child Welfare League of America
CWR	Child Welfare Reform

D

DD	Developmental Disability
DO	District Office
DOC	Department of Corrections
DOE	Department of Education
DOJ	Department of Justice
DOL	Department of Labor
DSMP	Diabetes Self-Management Program

E

EE	Extended Employment
EEOC	Equal Employment Opportunity Commission (US)
EI	Early Intervention
EITC	Earned Income Tax Credit
EOs	Executive Orders (from the Governor)

F

FAS	Fetal Alcohol Syndrome
FASD	Fetal Alcohol Spectrum Disorders
FCC	Federal Communications Commission
FFS	Fee-for-Service
FQHC	Federally Qualified Health Center
FSO	Family Support Organization
FT	Family Team
FTM	Family Team Meeting

G

GMO	Grants Management Officer
GPNFCSP	Grandparent National Family Caregiver Support Program

H

HCBS	Home and Community-Based Services
HDM	Home Delivered Meals
Health-EASE	Single entry system for health promotion/disease prevention information and coordination
HH	Hard of Hearing
HI	Hearing Impaired
HIPAA	Health Insurance Portability and Accountability Act
HIT	Health Information Technology
HIV	Human Immunodeficiency Virus
HMO	Health Maintenance Organization
HR	Human Resources
HRSA	Health Resources and Services Administration (US)
HUD	Department of Housing and Urban Development (US)

I

I/A or I/R	Information & Assistance/Referral
IADL(s)	Instrumental Activity (Activities) of Daily Living (e.g., making phone calls, writing checks)

IAS	Information and Assistance Services
ICC	Inspection, Compliance and Complaints
ICM	Intensive Case Management
ICMS	Integrated Case Management Services
ID	Intellectual Disabilities
IDDT	Integrated Dual Disorders Treatment
IDEA	Individuals with Disabilities Education Act
IDP	Intoxicated Driving Program
IDT	Interdisciplinary Team
IEP	Individual Education Plan
IFSS	Intensive Family Support Services
IHP	Individual Habilitation Plan
IOP	Intensive Outpatient
IPE	Individualized Plan for Employment
I&R	Information and Referral
ISP	Individual Service Plan

J

JCAHO	Joint Commission on Accreditation of Healthcare Organizations
JJC	Juvenile Justice Commission
JTPA	Job Training Partnership Act

L

LCADC	Licensed Clinical Alcohol and Drug Counselor
LIS	Licensing Information System
LOC	Level of Care
LOCI	Level of Care Index
LOS	Length of Stay or Level of Service
LRC	Licensed Residential Capacity or Learning Resource Center
LTC	Long Term Care
LTR	Long-Term Residential
LTSS	Long-Term Services and Supports

MA-PD	Medicare Advantage Plan (HMO, PPO) with a prescription drug benefit
MAST	Michigan Alcohol Screening Test
MAT	Medically Assisted Treatment
MD	Muscular Dystrophy
MDA	Muscular Dystrophy Association
MDSHC	Minimum Data Set for Home Care (standardized assessments for nursing home residents)
MDT	Multi-Disciplinary Team
MFP	Money Follows the Person
MICA	Mentally Ill Chemical Abuser
MIPPA	Medicare Improvements for Patients and Providers Act
MIOP	Methadone Intensive Outpatient
MM	Methadone Medication
MOU	Memorandum of Understanding
MRSS	Mobile Response and Stabilization Services
MS	Multiple Sclerosis

N

NAC-CHO	National Association of County & City Health Officials
NAMI	National Alliance for the Mentally Ill
NAPIS	National Aging Program Information System
NARA	National Association for Regulatory Administration
NASA-DAD	National Association of State Alcohol/Drug Abuse Directors
NASUAD	National Association of States United for Aging and Disabilities (formerly NASUA)
NBCAT	Needs-based Comprehensive Assessment Tool
NCQA	National Committee for Quality Assurance
NF	Nursing Facility
NFCSP	National Family Caregiver Support Program (Title III E of the Older Americans Act)
NI	Neurologically Impaired

NIAAA	National Institute on Alcohol Abuse and Alcoholism
NICHCY	National Information Center for Children and Youth with Disabilities
NIDA	National Institute on Drug Abuse
NIMAC	National Instructional Materials Access Center
NIMAS	National Instructional Materials Accessibility Standard
NOMs	National Outcome Measures
NOS	Not Otherwise Specified

O

OAA	Older Americans Act
OCD	Obsessive-Compulsive Disorder
OIG	Office of the Inspector General (US)
OPDF	Outpatient Drug Free
ORR	Office of Refugee Resettlement—U.S. Dept. of Health & Human Services, Administration for Children & Families
OT	Occupational Therapy

P

PA	Provider Agency
PAAD	Pharmaceutical Assistance to the Aged and Disabled
PAIMI	Protection and Advocacy for Individuals with Mental Illness
PAIR	Protection and Advocacy for Individual Rights
PAP	Pharmaceutical Assistance Program
PASRR	Pre-Admission Screening & Resident Review
PASS	Social Security Administration Plan to Achieve Self-Support
PATH	Projects for Assistance in Transition from Homelessness
PBC	Performance-Based Contracts
PBM	Performance-Based Management
PC	Partial Care
PCA	Personal Care Attendant or Personal Care Assistance
PDD	Pervasive Developmental Disorder
PDP	Prescription Drug Plan

PEIS	Prevention & Early Intervention Services
PFA	Psychological First Aid
PIP	Program Improvement Plan
PMO	Program Management Officer
PNA	Personal Needs Allowance
PPMD	Postpartum Mood Disorder
PPSD	Postpartum Stress Disorder
PRO	Peer Review Organization
PT	Physical Therapy
PTSD	Posttraumatic Stress Disorder
PVC	Polyvinyl Chloride

Q

QA	Quality Assurance
QAC	Quality Assurance Coordinator
QAS	Quality Assurance Specialist
QCMR	Quarterly Contract Monitoring Report
QI	Quality Indicator
QMP	Quality Management & Planning
QSR	Quality Service Review

R

RDS	Resource Development Specialist
RFI	Request for Information
RFP	Request for Proposal
RFQ	Request for Qualifications
RHCF	Residential Health Care Facility
RHHI	Regional Home Health Intermediary
RSD	Reflexive Sympathetic Dystrophy

S

SAI	Substance Abuse Initiative
SAMHSA	Substance Abuse and Mental Health Services Administration
SAMS	Social Assistance Management System (a software program owned/operated by Harmony)

SAPT	Substance Abuse Prevention and Treatment
SASSI	Substance Abuse Subtle Screening Inventory
SCI	Spinal Cord Injury
SCR	Statewide Centralized Registry
SDM	Structured Decision Making
SE or **SES**	Supportive Employment Services
SHIP	State Health Insurance Assistance Program
SILC	Statewide Independent Living Council
SLMB	Specified Low-Income Medicare Beneficiary
SNAP	Special Needs Advocate for Parents
SNAP	Supplemental Nutrition Assistance Program (food stamps)
SRT	Special Response Team
SSA	Social Security Administration
SSDI	Social Security Disability Income
SSI	Supplemental Security Income
STR	Short-Term Residential
STS	Speech to Speech
SUA	State Unit on Aging

T

TANF	Temporary Assistance for Needy Families
TBI	Traumatic Brain Injury
TBIF	Traumatic Brain Injury Fund
TDD	Telecommunications Device for the Deaf
TEE	Thorough and Efficient Education
TLJC	Time Limited Job Coaching
TO	Table of Organization
TT	Text Telephone
TTY	Teletypewriter

U

UAP	University Affiliated Program
UCC	Uniform Construction Code
UCPA	United Cerebral Palsy Association
UFC	Uniform Fire Code

UIR	Unusual Incident Report
UR	Utilization Review
USAID	United States Agency for International Development
USF	Universal Service Fund

V

VA	Veterans' Administration
VI	Visually Impaired
VMHS	Veterans Mental Health Services
VRS	Vocational Rehabilitation Services

W

WIC	Supplemental Nutrition Program for Women, Infants, and Children
WIOA	Workforce Innovation and Opportunity Act
WRAP	Wellness and Recovery Action Plan

Y

YAP	Youth Advocate Program
YCM	Youth Case Management

APPENDIX C
SAMPLE RESUME

Pat Jones, MSW, LMSW
555 Main Street, Apt. 2A
Anytown, NY 10069
555-555-5555
pat.jones@gmail.com

PROFESSIONAL SUMMARY

I am an enthusiastic bilingual social work professional seeking a position working with children or families. I have experience working in trauma-informed settings and advocating for social justice.

EDUCATION

Master's Degree in Social Work | May 2023

State University of New York

Bachelor of Arts, Psychology | May 2021

State University of New York

EXPERIENCE

Social Work Intern | September 2022-May 2023

Human Services Agency, New York, New York

- Conducted initial assessments of new clients and worked with experienced staff to identify relevant services.
- Managed a caseload of five to seven individual clients and led two groups focusing on recovery.
- Participated in weekly supervision sessions.
- Documented client sessions and reviewed client files regularly to evaluate progress.

Social Work Intern | September 2021-May 2022

Boys and Girls Club, Anytown, New York

- Worked closely with experienced staff to run an after-school program.
- Met with children individually who were referred by the neighborhood school to help identify needs.
- Observed and participated in social skills groups throughout internship.
- Assisted with administrative work, including making referrals and documenting client progress.

SKILLS

Fluent in Spanish—reading, writing, speaking | Completed trauma-informed seminar with licensed social workers at Human Services Agency (November 2022) | Excellent written and oral communication skills.

REFERENCES

CHAPTER 4

Association for College & Research Libraries. (2015). *Framework for information literacy for higher education*. American Library Association. http://www.ala.org/acrl/files/issues/infolit/framework.pdf

Harrington, M. R. (2009). Information literacy and research-intensive graduate students: Enhancing the role of research librarians. *Behavioral & Social Sciences Librarian*, *28*(4), 179–201. https://doi.org/10.1080/01639260903272778

CHAPTER 5

American Psychological Association (APA). (2020). *Publication manual of the American Psychological Association* (7th ed.). https://doi.org/10.1037/0000165-000

CHAPTER 7

lumen. (n.d.). *Introduction: Critical thinking, reading, & writing*. College Reading and Writing. https://courses.lumenlearning.com/suny-esc-introtocollege readingandwriting/chapter/introduction-critical-reading-writing/

INDEX

Note: **Bold** page numbers refer to tables and *italic* page numbers refer to figures.

abbreviations 3
acronyms 47
Activities of Daily Living (ADL) 133
addiction services 42
Addiction Severity Index (ASI) 134
Addiction Technology Transfer
    Center (ATTC) 134
adjectives 88–9
administration 25
Administration on Aging (AoA) 133
Administration for Community
    Living (ACL) 133
Administrative Office of the Courts
    (AOC) 133
Administrative Order (AO) 133
Adult Day Care (ADC) 133
Adult Family Care (AFC) 133
Adult Protective Services (APS) 133
advocacy 25, 59
age 25, 89
Agency for Health Care Policy and
    Research (AHCPR) 133
AGIS (AssistGuide Information
    System) County SAMS Adminis-
    trator (ACSA) 133
AI *see* artificial intelligence (AI) 94
AIDS (Acquired Immune Deficiency
    Syndrome) 133; *see also* HIV
Alcohol and Drug Abuse Data
    System (ADADS) 133

Alcohol and Other Drugs
    (AOD) 133
Alzheimer's Adult Day Services
    Program (AADSP) 133
American Association for the
    Treatment of Opioid Dependence
    (AATOD) 133
American Civil Liberties Union
    (ACLU) 133
American Methadone Treatment
    Association (AMTA) 133
American Psychiatric Association 77
American Psychological Association
    (APA) 126, 128; 7ᵗʰ Edition format
    2–3, 7, 8, 14, 18, 21, 71, 75–6,
    78–81, 83, 86, 87, 89, 91, 124–31;
    citation program software 93;
    Citation Reference Machine 82;
    Common Reference Examples
    Guide 92; grammar 92; guid-
    ance 92; *Manual* 3; Online Guide
    to Bias-Free Language 87;
    plagiarism 92; punctuation 92;
    Student Paper Checklist 86, 92;
    Student Paper SetUp Guide 82–3,
    85–6, 92; Style and Grammar
    Guidelines 92; website 82; writing
    checklist 91; writing style 75–93;
    see also citations; references;
    software; Student Paper Setup

Guide; style; subject headings; tables; websites
American Recovery and Reinvestment Act 2009 (ARRA) 133
American Sign Language (ASL) 134
American Society of American Addictions (ASAA) 134
Americans with Disabilities Act (ADA) 133
Amyotrophic Lateral Sclerosis (ALS) 133
anchors 119
Angelo State University 73
Antioch University 83, 92
anxiety 3, 94–7; assessment of work 97; deadlines 95; exercises 102–3; idea-gathering 95–6; negative past experiences 96; self-belief 96
APA *see* American Psychological Association (APA)
Area Agency on Aging (AAA) 133
Area Plan Contract (APC) 133
artificial intelligence (AI) 94; software 104–5
assignments 2; *see also* class assignments
Assisted Living (AL) 133
Assistive Listening Device (ALD) 133
Association for College & Research Libraries 65
Association of Social Work Boards 32
Attention Deficit Disorder (ADD) 133
Attention Deficit Hyperactivity Disorder (ADHD) 133
attributions 30
Author 103
autism 5
AutoRecover 70

bias-free language 6, 87–90; adjectives, use of 88–9; age and 89; culture and 90; gender 89; gender pronouns 90; labels 88–9; nouns, use of 88–9; respectfulness 89; sexual orientation 89; social work treatment or research, participation

in 90; socioeconomic status 89; specificity, levels of 87–8
bibliographies 17, 65, 70–1, 78
Blackboard 23
Blind and Visually Impaired (BVI) 134
Board of Social Services (BSS) 134
books 67
Boolean operators 74
brainstorming 9
business letters 62

calendars 14, 98
Canvas 23
Care Management Organization (CMO) 135
career research 67
case notes 27–8
Case Practice Specialist (CPS) 135
case studies 7
Center for Independence Living (CIL) 134
Centers for Medicare and Medicaid Services (CMS) 135
Cerebral Palsy (CP) 135
Certificate of Need (CN) 135
Certified Alcohol and Drug Counselor (CADC) 134
Certified Nursing Assistant (CNA) 135
charts 31
Chemical Dependence (CD) 134
Centers for Disease Control and Prevention (CDC/CDCP) 134
Child Family Service Review (CFSR) 134
Child Family Team (CFT) 134
Child Protection Specialist (CPS) 135
Child Study Team (CST) 135
Child Welfare League of America (CWLA) 135
Child Welfare Reform (CWR) 135
Children of Substance Abusers (COSA) 135
children: child custody cases 27; language use 89; parenting skills **87**

Children's Health Insurance Program (CHIP) 134
Chronic Disease Self-Management Program (CDSMP) 134
citations 2, 7, 20, 22, 70–1, 75–6, 128; common types **77**; program software 93; rules 76–7; tools 67; websites 81–3
civic development agencies 29
class assignments: checklist 24; formatting of papers 20–1; Generalist Practice Courses 8; organizational skills 10–13; proofreading 21–3; reading the assignment 7–8; rough drafts 19–20; seven step approach 7, 13; Social Policy Courses 8–9; submission of 23; time management 10–15; writing for 6–24; *see also* scholarship
clients: assessments 2; confidentiality 118; problems 12
clinical notes 2
clinical social work 25
Clinical Social Work Association 32
Code of Federal Regulations (CFR) 134
Cognitive Behavioral Therapy (CBT) 115, 134
collaboration models 2–3, 122
Commission on Accreditation of Rehabilitation Facilities (CARF) 134
common writing challenges 3, 94–107; general writing resources 106; time management resources 101–2, 106–7; writing checklist 105; *see also* anxiety; artificial intelligence (AI); deadlines; time management; writing software
Communication Assisted Realtime Translation (CART) 134
communication skills: effective 2; formal *vs* informal 4, 47; importance of 1, 2; professional 1; types of communication 2; *see also* culturally responsive

communication; forms of communication; written communication
Community Care Residence (CCR) 134
Community Care Waiver (CCW) 134
Community Living Program (CLP) 135
community organization 25; agencies 27
community referral 45
community service interventions 35
Comprehensive Personal Care Home (CPCH) 135
confidentiality 118
Congregate Housing Services Program (CHSP) 134
Consumer Assistance Program (CAP) 134
Continuing Care Retirement Communities (CCRC) 134
Continuous Quality Improvement (CQI) 135
Contract Management System (CMS) 135
Controlled Dangerous Substance (CDS) 134
Cornell College, Mt Vernon 122
Council on Accreditation of Residential Facilities (CARF) 134
Council on Social Work Education 32
countertransference 34–5
County Boards of Social Services (CBOSS) 134
County Interagency Coordinating Council (CIACC) 134
County Welfare Agencies 134, 135; *see also* Board of Social Services (BSS)
cover letters 53–5; examples 54–5
critical comprehension 122
Critical Incident Management Unit (CIMU) 135
critical reading 3, 108–22; building skills 121–2; definition of 108;

reading policy papers 111–12; reading practice articles 115–16; textbook reading 110–11; *see also* research articles
critical thinking 3, 108–22; building skills 121–2; definition of 108
critical writing 108–22; additional creative suggestions 118; building skills 121–2; creative nature of 116–18; creativity through multiple perspectives 117–18; freestyle written client referral 119; 'how-to' paper 118; informative nature of 116–18; reactive nature of 116–18; types of 109; writing reports 118–20
cultural competence 2
culturally responsive communication 5–6; bias-free language 90
Curriculum Vitae (CV) *see* resumes

Dartmouth University 101, 107
databases 16, 54, 68; research skills 74
deadlines 3, 7, 97–101; calendars 98; estimates 98; meeting 97–9; positivity 99, 101; prioritization 100; resources 98; schedule tables **99**; small tasks 98; 'to-do' lists 98; work schedules **99**; *see also* time management
dementia 89
demographics: client 34
Department of Corrections (DOC) 135
Department of Education (DOE) 135
Department of Justice (DOJ) 135
Department of Labor (DOL) 135
depression 28, 119
Developmental Disability (DD) 135
Dewey Decimal System 73
Diabetes Self-Management Program (DSMP) 135
disabilities: developmental 25; language use 5, 42, 88–9; reasonable accommodations 98
disagreements 30

discrimination: employment 27; gender 88
District Office (DO) 135
diversity 34–5, 54
doctoral students 2
document storage 69–72
Dropbox 71–3
drug policy 7

Early Intervention (EI) 135
Earned Income Tax Credit (EITC) 135
EBSCO 16
education sites 42
electronic records 31
email 4, 47–50; guidelines for emailing professors 60; thank-you 57–8; workplace 61
emojis 4, 47, 51
employment 78; discrimination 27; employee assistance 25
EndNote 81, 93
Entrepreneur.com 61
environmental groups 42
Equal Employment Opportunity Commission (EEOC) 135
errors *see* grammar; punctuation; spelling
essay topics 7
ethics: dilemmas 34–5; guidelines 32
ethnicity 88
Executive Orders (EOs) 135
Extended Employment (EE) 135

families: wellbeing of 11; writing differences 40–1
Family Support Organization (FSO) 136
Family Team Meeting (FTM) 136
Federal Communications Commission (FCC) 136
Federally Qualified Health Center (FQHC) 136
Fee-for-Service (FFS) 136
feedback 9
Fetal Alcohol Syndrome (FAS) 136
figures 129; APA style *131*

final recommendations 129
FocusWriter 103
food stamps *see* Supplemental Nutrition Assistance Program (SNAP)
forms of communication 46–64; audience 46; business letters 62; checklist 60; conciseness 47; cover letters 63; informativeness 47; miscellaneous letters 59; mode of communication 47; perception of messages 47; proofreading messages 47; rationale for writing 46–7; self-presentation 46–7; thank-you letters 64; Zoom meeting etiquette 61; *see also* email; job applications; letters; online meetings; resumes; text messages (DMs)
fraud 27
fundraising 35

gender 89; discrimination 88; identity 88–9; language use 88–9; pronouns 89; *see also* sexual orientation
GIFs 51
Glassdoor 63
Google 2, 110; Docs 65, 70–1, 80–1, 83, 85, 103; Drive 72–3; Meet 51; Scholar 17
government information 67
grammar 3–5, 21, 47–9, 91–2
Grammarly 61, 85, 105; Basic 82–3, 103; Premium 82–3, 103
Grandparent National Family Caregiver Support Program (GP NFCSP) 136
Grants Management Office (GMO) 136
groups: 'closed' 28; 'open door' 28

Hard of Hearing (HH) 136
Harvard Business Review 63
Health-EASE system 136
Health Information Technology (HIT) 136
Health Insurance Portability and Accountability Act (HIPAA) 42, 136
Health Maintenance Organization (HMO) 136
Health Resources and Services Administration (HRSA) 136
healthcare 25, 26
Hearing Impaired (HI) 136
HIV (Human Immunodeficiency Virus) 136; *see also* AIDS
Home and Community-Based Services (HCBS) 136
Home Delivered Meals (HDM) 136
homelessness 45, 59, 78
hospitalization 120
Housing and Urban Development, US (HUD) 136
housing: conditions 119; supervised 39
HuffPost 62
Human Resources (HR) 136
Hygger Project Management 107
hyperlinks 130

ideas, structuring of 3
idioms 6
immigration 7, 67
Indeed 61, 64
Individual Education Plan (IEP) 137
Individual Habilitation Plan (IHP) 137
Individual Service Plan (ISP) 137
Individualized Plan for Employment (IPE) 137
Individuals with Disabilities Education Act (IDEA) 137
Information and Assistance (I/A) 137
information literacy 65–9; libraries and 73–4
Information and Referral (I/R) 137
Inspection, Compliance and Complaints (ICC) 137
Instrumental Activity (Activities) of Daily Living (IADLs) 136
insurance cases 27, 28
Integrated Case Management Services (ICMS) 137

Integrated Dual Disorders Treatment (IDDT) 137
Intellectual Disabilities (ID) 137
Intensive Case Management (ICM) 137
Intensive Family Support Services (IFSS) 137
Intensive Outpatient (IOP) 137
Interdisciplinary Team (IDT) 137
interlibrary loans 73
international social work 25
internship 25–45; additional exercises 44; areas of practice 25; assessment 34, 36; books 44; client assessments 37–8; fields of practice, technical aspects of 26–7; generalist year chart **33**; macro-systems 38; MSW Journal Recording Column Chart **3**; process recordings and journals 32–7; project/activity description 36; reports 39; self- reflection 34, 36–7; specialization year chart **35**; technical terms, use of 26–7; technology and writing for 32; writing checklist 43; *see also* note-taking; referrals; reports; resumes; writing differences
Intoxicated Driving Program (IDP) 137

job applications 53–8; cover letters 53–5; resumes 56–7; thank-you emails 57–8; *see also* resumes
Joint Commission on Accreditation of Healthcare Organizations (JCAHO) 137
journals 16–17, 32–7; articles 67–8; full-text searches 68; PDF searches 68; peer reviewed articles 67–8, 73; publication date of articles 68; search terms 68; usefulness of 35
justice: corrective 25
Juvenile Justice Commission (JJC) 137

labels 88–9
language: academic expectation 128; cultural considerations 5–6;

disabilities 5; invented 4; model paper 127–8; professional social work 96; race 5; standard 4; *see also* bias-free language; grammar; idioms; pronoun use; punctuation; slang; spelling
Learning Management Systems 23
Learning Resource Center (LRC) 137
legislation 59
Length of Stay (LOS) 137
letters: business 62; miscellaneous 59; thank you 64; *see also* cover letters
Level of Care (LOC) 137
Level of Service (LOS) 137
levels of specificity: concept of 87–8
libraries 17, 65–9; documents and 72–3; information literacy 73–4; interlibrary loans 69; librarians 66; locating documents 72–3; schools 2; services and events 67; visits 66; websites 66
LibreOffice Writer 103
Licensed Clinical Alcohol and Drug Counselor (LCADC) 137
Licensed Residential Capacity (LRC) 137
Licensing Information System (LIS) 137
literacy *see* information literacy
logs 27, 31; activity notes 29
Long-Term Care (LTC) 137
Long-Term Residential (LTR) 137
Long-Term Services and Supports (LTSS) 137
Lou Gehrig's Disease *see* Amyotrophic Lateral Sclerosis (ALS)
lumen learning 121

Mac Operating System 103
malpractice 27
management 25
marital discord 78
Master of Social Work (MSW) 2, 31, 54; journal recording column chart **36**

Medically Assisted Treatment
(MAT) 138
Medicare Advantage Plan
(MA-PD) 138
Medicare Improvements for Patients
and Providers Act (MIPPA) 138
Memorandum of Understanding
(MOU) 138
memos 33
Mendeley Cite 81, 93
mental health 119; agencies 39;
clinical social work 25; substance
abuse social work 25; *see also*
severe mental illness (SMI)
Mentally Ill Chemical Abuser
(MICA) 138
Methadone Intensive Outpatient
(MIOP) 138
Methadone Medication (MM) 138
Michigan Alcohol Screening Test
(MAST) 138
Microsoft 62; Edge 93; Office 54;
Teams 51; Word 65, 69–70, 80–1,
85, 93, 103–4
Mindtools 106
Minimum Data Set for Home Care
(MDSHC) 138
Mobile Response and Stabilization
Services (MRSS) 138
Money Follows the Person (MFP) 138
Monster 63
Montclair State University 34, 35,
37, 74
Multi-Disciplinary Team (MDT) 138
Multiple Sclerosis (MS) 138
Muscular Dystrophy (MD) 138
Muse, The 64

National Aging Program Information
System (NAPIS) 138
National Alliance for the Mentally Ill
(NAMI) 138
National Association for Regulatory
Administration (NARA) 138
National Association of County &
City Health Officials
(NAC-CHO) 138

National Association of Social Work
(NASW) 25, 32, 39; Code of
Ethics 44
National Association of State
Alcohol/Drug Abuse Directors
(NASA-DAD) 138
National Association of States United
for Aging and Disabilities
(NASUAD) 138
National Committee for Quality
Assurance (NCQA) 138
National Family Caregiver Support
Program (NFCSP) 138
National Information Center for
Children and Youth with
Disabilities (NICHCY) 139
National Institute on Alcohol Abuse
and Alcoholism (NIAAA) 139
National Institute on Drug Abuse
(NIDA) 139
National Instructional Materials
Access Center (NIMAC) 139
National Instructional Materials
Accessibility Standard
(NIMAS) 139
National Organization of Social
Workers 76, **77**
National Outcome Measures
(NOMs) 139
Needs-based Comprehensive
Assessment Tool (NBCAT) 138
Neurologically Impaired (NI) 138
New Hampshire University 73
New York Times 16
News.com 60
news resources 67
newspapers 67
Nexis Uni 16
Northern Illinois University Center
for Innovative Teaching 60
Northwestern University
Libraries 73
Not Otherwise Specified (NOS) 139
note-taking 17–18, 27–32, 122;
attributions 30; case notes 27–8;
disagreements 30; identifying
others 29; log activity notes 29;

making changes 31; pronouns 30; self- identification 29–30
nouns 88–9
Nursing Facility (NF) 138
nursing homes 42

Obsessive-Compulsive Disorder (OCD) 139
occupation assistance 25
Occupational Therapy (OT) 139
Office of the Inspector General, US (OIG) 139
Office of Refugee Resettlement, US (ORR) 139
official documents *see* note-taking
Older Americans Act (OAA) 139
OneDrive 70
online meetings 51–3; 'log in and leave' 52–3; minimal distractions 51–2; multitasking, avoidance of 52; professionalism in 52; technological operation 52; quiet environment 51–2
organizational activism 35
organizational skills 7, 10–13, 54
outlines 10–13; benefits of 10
Outpatient Drug Free (OPDF) 139
outside readings 76
Oxford Royale Academy 73

page numbers 18
paragraphs: headings (*see* subject headings); numbers 18
paraphrasing 76–7, 128–9
Partial Care (PC) 139
Peer Review Organization (PRO) 140
Perdue University: Online Writing Lab (OWL) 82, 86, 92, 95, 101, 106–7
Performance-Based Contracts (PBC) 139
Performance-Based Management (PBM) 139
Personal Care Assistance (PCA) 139
Personal Care Attendant (PCA) 139

personal communication 128–9
Personal Needs Allowance (PNA) 140
personal problems 11–12
Pervasive Developmental Disorder (PDD) 139
Pharmaceutical Assistance to the Aged and Disabled (PAAD) 139
Pharmaceutical Assistance Program (PAP) 139
photography 118, 121
Physical Therapy (PT) 140
plagiarism 23, 74, 75, 83, 92
policy 35; planning 25; reading papers 111–12
Political Science Guide 122
politics 25
Postpartum Mood Disorder (PPMD) 140
Postpartum Stress Disorder (PPSD) 140
Posttraumatic Stress Disorder (PTSD) 140
Pre-Admission Screening & Resident Review (PASRR) 139
Prescription Drug Plan (PDP) 139
Prevention & Early Intervention Services (PEIS) 140
prisoners 42
privacy rights 118, 121
process recordings 32–7; function of 32; templates 32–4
procrastination 97; definition of 94
professional writing 3
Program Improvement Plan (PIP) 140
Program Management Officer (PMO) 140
Projects for Assistance in Transition from Homelessness (PATH) 139
pronouns 6, 11, 29, 30, 89
proofreading 7, 13, 15, 21–4, 47, 49, 56, 58, 60
Protection and Advocacy for Individuals with Mental Illness (PAIMI) 139

Protection and Advocacy for Individual Rights (PAIR) 139
Provider Agency (PA) 139
PsychINFO 16
psychodynamic therapy 78, 115
Psychological First Aid (PFA) 140
psychosocial reports 7
public welfare 25
Publication Manual 79
punctuation 3, 5, 21, 47, 49, 87, 92
Purdue Online Writing Lab 62
PVC (Polyvinyl Chloride) 140

Quality Assurance (QA) 140
Quality Assurance Coordinator (QAC) 140
Quality Assurance Specialist (QAS) 140
Quality Management & Planning (QMP) 140
Quality Service Review (QSR) 140
Quarterly Contract Monitoring Report Quality Indicator (QCMR) 140
quotation marks 18

race 5; language use 88
references 44, 128, 130; examples 79–80; font 79; format 79; hanging style 78; organization 93; page 78–80; websites 81–3
referrals 38–9; forms, examples of 45
Reflexive Sympathetic Dystrophy (RSD) 140
Regional Home Health Intermediary (RHHI) 140
religion 88
reports: internships 38–9; guidelines to report writing 45; macro-assignments 2; writing 118–20
Request for Information (RFI) 140
Request for Proposal (RFP) 140
Request for Qualifications (RFQ) 140
research 25; articles see research articles; guides 66–7; methods and processes 73

research articles 112–14; discussion 113; introduction 113; methods 113; references 113; results 113; see also critical reading
Residential Health Care Facility (RHCF) 140
Resource Development Specialist (RDS) 140
respectfulness 89
resumes 56–7, 63; brevity of 56–7; contact information 144; editing 57; education history 144; entry-level jobs 3; experience 144–5; professional summary 144; relevance 57; sample 144–5; skills 145; up-to-date information 57
rough drafts 19–20

Saint Leo University 103, 106
schedules 14–15
schizophrenia 77–8; antipsychotic treatment 78; bibliographies 17; books 16; databases 16; definition of 15–16; journals 16–17; note-taking 17–18; peer-reviewed articles 15–16; reading material 17; reports 16; risks associated with 78; scholarship 15–18; sources 16–17; symptoms of 77; see also Google Scholar
school social work 25, 26
Scribus 103
Scrivener 103
search engines 2; see also Google
Sembly AI 61
sentence structure 4
sessions: accomplishments 34–6; goals and objectives 34–5; outcomes 34; plans 34–6; supervision: questions for 34–6
Seven Steps of Assignment Writing 7, 13
severe mental illness (SMI) 77
sexual orientation 88, 89; see also gender
Short-Term Residential (STR) 141

Simple Texting 62
slang 6
smartphones 4
Social Assistance Management System (SAMS) 140
social media 4
Social Policy Courses 8–9
Social Security Administration (SSA) 141
Social Security Administration Plan to Achieve Self-Support (PASS) 139
Social Security Disability Income (SSDI) 141
social service agencies 111
Social Work Abstracts 16
social work treatment or research 90
socioeconomic status (SES) 88, 89
software 80–1; citations 93; EndNote 81; Mendeley Cite 81; Zotero 80–1; *see also* artificial intelligence (AI); word processing software; writing software
Special Needs Advocate for Parents (SNAP) 141
Special Response Team (SRT) 141
specificity, levels of 87–8
Specified Low-Income Medicare Beneficiary (SLMB) 141
Speech to Speech (STS) 141
spelling 3, 4, 21–2, 47–8, 69, 87, 91
Spinal Cord Injury (SCI) 141
State Health Insurance Assistance Program (SHIP) 141
State Unit on Aging (SUA) 141
Statewide Centralized Registry (SCR) 141
Statewide Independent Living Council (SILC) 141
statistics 67
stickers 51
Structured Decision Making (SDM) 141
Student Paper Setup Guide 82–3, 85–6, 92
style: elements of 86–7; guides 7; model example 124–31

subject headings 83–4; guide to formatting paragraph headings **84**; heading level use, tips on 83–4; paragraph headings 83
substance abuse 25, 119
Substance Abuse Initiative (SAI) 140
Substance Abuse and Mental Health Services Administration (SAMHSA) 140
Substance Abuse Prevention and Treatment (SAPT) 141
Substance Abuse Subtle Screening Inventory (SASSI) 141
Supplemental Nutrition Assistance Program (SNAP) 141
Supplemental Nutrition Program for Women, Infants, and Children (WIC) 142
Supplemental Security Income (SSI) 141
Supportive Employment Services (SES) 141
systems theory 46

Table of Organization (TO) 141
tables 85–6, 129; APA style **131;** mixed words and numbers 86
technology *see* books; document storage; information literacy; journals; libraries; research; word processing software
Technology in Social Work Practice 32
TechRadar Pro 103, 106
Telecommunications Device for the Deaf (TDD) 141
teleconferencing 51–2
Teletypewriter (TTY) 141
Temporary Assistance for Needy Families (TANF) 141
Texas A&M University 106
text messages (DMs) 4, 47, 50–1, 51; professional 62
Text Telephone (TT) 141
Thorough and Efficient Education (TEE) 141

Time Limited Job Coaching (TLJC) 141
time management 7, 10–15, 97–101, 122; mapping ideas 102; planning 101; research 102; resources 106–7; sharing ideas 102; time organization, concept of 3, 99–101; time resources, uniqueness of 100; *see also* deadlines
TopResume.com 61
Traumatic Brain Injury (TBI) 141
Traumatic Brain Injury Fund (TBIF) 141
treatment therapy 115
TurnItIn 23

Uniform Construction Code (UCC) 141
Uniform Fire Code (UFC) 141
United Cerebral Palsy Association (UCPA) 141
United States Agency for International Development (USAID) 142
Universal Service Fund (USF) 142
University Affiliated Program (UAP) 141
University of North Carolina 121
University of the Potomac 61
Unusual Incident Report (UIR) 142
Utilization Review (UR) 142

Veterans' Administration (VA) 142
Veterans Mental Health Services (VMHS) 142
video recordings 33, 118
Visually Impaired (VI) 142; *see also* Blind and Visually Impaired (BVI)
Vocational Rehabilitation Services (VRS) 142
voice recordings 33, 118, 121

websites 81–3; Antioch University, example paper from 83, 92; APA 7th Edition Style 82, 92

welfare: public 25
well-written paper: model of 3, 123–31
Wellness and Recovery Action Plan (WRAP) 142
Western Michigan University 37
WIC *see* Supplemental Nutrition Program for Women, Infants, and Children
Wikipedia 16
Windows Operating System 103
word processing software 69–72; Dropbox 71–2; Google Docs 70–1; Microsoft Word 69–70
Workforce Innovation and Opportunity Act (WIOA) 142
Write-Monkey 103
writing differences 39–43; community settings 41–2; couples 40–1; families 40–1; groups 41; individuals 40–1; organizations 42–3
writing skills: drafting process 2; editing process 2; partners, use of 1; professional *see* professional writing; poor, effect of 1; strategies 2; *see also* common writing challenges
writing software 103–4; important note 103–4; tips 103
written communication: importance of 1–2, 4–5; *see also* class assignments

Yeshiva University 8
Yonis, Amina 122
Youth Advocate Program (YAP) 142
Youth Case Management (YCM) 142

ZipRecruiter 63
Zoom 51, 52, 54, 58, 60; meeting etiquette 61
Zotero 80–1, 93

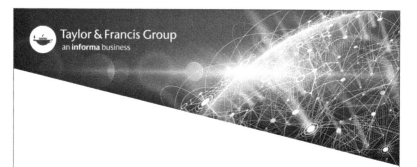